David O'Malley SDB

CW00514971

A young adult's guide to life

Support for young adults from the Salesian tradition and Catholic perspective

Don Bosco
Publications

Don Bosco Publications
Thornleigh House, Sharples Park, Bolton BL1 6PQ
United Kingdom

ISBN 978-1-916546-03-5
©Don Bosco Publications 2023
©David O'Malley SDB

The moral rights of the author have been asserted

All rights reserved. No part of this publication may be reproduced, stored in a retrieval system or transmitted in any form or by any means without the prior permission in writing of Don Bosco Publications. Enquiries concerning reproduction and requests for permissions should be sent to The Manager, Don Bosco Publications, at the address above.

Front cover image: @Unsplash/chang-duong-Sj0iMtq_Z4w
Page vii: @Unsplash/yapo-zhou-YIPSx8PFi9s
Page 10: @Unsplash/robin-schreiner-7y4858E8PfA
Page 43: @Unsplash/vincent-van-zalinge-PS8miM4xR1I
Page 89: @Unsplash/emanuel-haas-5GIozEQXuhY

Printed in Malta by Melita Press

MIX
Paper from
responsible sources
FSC® C004116

Contents

Salesian Beatitudes

Blessed are those who receive, with gratitude, all of life as a gift.

Blessed are those who find a happy balance in daily living.

Blessed are those who are energetic in working for a more just and caring society.

Blessed are those who have the gentleness of Christ, the Good Shepherd.

Blessed are those who are willing to open their hearts to others with confidence and trust.

Blessed are those who are optimistic about the goodness in others.

Blessed are those who discover cheerfulness as a way to live the Gospel.

Blessed are those who have concern for the vulnerable and the poor.

Introduction

Speaking to the administrators of the Catholic Church in Rome, Pope Francis quoted Cardinal Martini, who, towards the end of his life, said that:

The Church is two hundred years behind the times. Why is she not shaken up? Are we afraid? Fear, instead of courage? Yet faith is the Church's foundation. Faith, confidence, courage ... Only love conquers weariness.[1]

This short guide for young adults is offered in love: love for young adults as they meet a complex and challenging world, and love for the Church that knows that it needs to change and feels fearful of that change. This book is part of a bridge between a hesitant Church and a new generation that is sometimes frustrated with their experience of being Church. It encourages an atmosphere of faith in the Gospel and an openness to exploration. This book is an encouragement to trust the treasury of the Church, not the money but the tradition of Gospel and Sacraments, the living tradition of prayer and the service of the poor.

It is easy to let the present-day media paint an unbalanced picture of our Catholic Church. It is a little-known fact that our Catholic Church is the largest non-state charity in the world. It serves people the world over through education, health, development, and disaster relief. Even in developed countries Catholic communities can always be seen quietly serving the common good as a sign of God's love for all people. So, whilst many young adults may be disheartened

1   Pope Francis, *Christmas Greetings to The Roman Curia*, Clementine Hall, December 21, 2019.

and angered by the shadows of abuse and clericalism that paralyse the energy of the Gospel, they must also become proud of the living Gospel acted out by millions of Catholics all over the world. The love and faithfulness of such Catholics will renew our Church from the laity to the hierarchy. There will be years of growing pains, tensions, uncertainty, but today's young adults will be the generation that begins to reshape our Church. We, Salesians, hope that this book will support young adults as they deepen their Gospel faith and find new ways to live it and share it in the future.

Perhaps the last words should be those of Pope Francis:

> We, the women, and men of the Church, we are in the middle of a love story: each of us is a link in this chain of love. And if we do not understand this, we have understood nothing of what the Church really is.[2]

---

2   Pope Francis, *Homily*, Chapel of the Casa Santa Marta, April 24, 2013.

SECTION I

Salesian Spirituality

Salesian Spirituality

The spirituality that inspires this book is called "Salesian". It is a heart-centred way of looking at life and relating to God in ordinary experience. It is optimistic, gentle, cheerful and deeply contemplative in the middle of ordinary life. It is a great way to live the Gospel in practical and heart-felt ways. Francis de Sales began this school of spirituality during the reformation in the sixteenth century. When others were encouraging persecution of Protestants or Catholics, Francis was encouraging gentleness and understanding. When others were saying that God could only be found in Sacrament or in the words of the Bible, Francis was encouraging people to find God in ordinary life, among the pots and pans and in working life. His writing and preaching as Bishop of Geneva was the birth of a spirituality which now bears his name.

Don Bosco was a priest who began to work with young people in Turin at the start of the industrial revolution in the nineteenth century. He adopted Francis de Sales as his patron and developed that spirituality for a different era and for work with the young and the poor. You will find a many more quotes from Don Bosco and from Francis de Sales later in this book. A key quotation from Don Bosco is this:

> Young people not only need to be loved, but they also need to know that they are loved.

Loving kindness is at the centre of Don Bosco's approach to life. He believed that a gentle and optimistic approach to people opened hearts, built up confidence and increased joy in life. In order to do that, a Salesian needs to get out of their own world and understand the others world. Which means moving the centre of your life away from yourself and closer to God and to the other person.

Salesian Themes

Here are some Salesian themes which you may already be experiencing in your life, and some that may challenge you to grow:

- **Gentleness**—The care and sensitivity of the Good Shepherd, Jesus.
- **Optimism**—Belief that God is with us all so all will eventually be well.
- **Presence**—Awareness of myself, others and God in a communion of people.

- **Loving Kindness**—Compassion and generosity in trusting others and oneself.
- **Gratitude**—Being able to count one's blessings and thank others.
- **Meaning**—Reflecting prayerfully on what life teaches every day.

Loving Kindness

Don Bosco put loving kindness at the heart of his way of working, and he was following a long tradition in doing so. Buddhism uses the word '*metta*' for loving kindness. The original Judaic scripture uses the word '*chesed*' (pronounced *hessed*) and even Homer, writing in about 800BCE, used the word '*agape*' which was later adopted by Christians to describe loving kindness. This cardinal virtue of the Catholic Church, often described as charity, is a natural healer, a builder of relationships and a sign of God's love alive in people. So, isn't it surprising that such a vital virtue is under threat in our culture and even in our family lives?

Our culture favours the rugged, independent individual, the soloist hero who needs no other person. Our homes and families can become so busy and fragmented that kindness is overshadowed by personal success. The business world can take a narrow view of work, leaving kindness in the shadows as an optional by-product of the workplace. Those who help others are often seen as 'soft'. Helping a friend who is struggling, for example, will often raise eyebrows before applause from others. Empathy is being overwhelmed by competition or success, and kindness could become a forgotten virtue.

But just because kindness is in the shadows does not mean that it is absent, far from it. Our experience is full of acts of random kindness that make life worth living. Motorists breaking down on the road, people short of bus fare and those involved in accidents all witness to the existence of a web of loving kindness beneath the surface of our busy lives. These acts of kindness seed our lives with hope and yet they rarely make their way into the newspapers that prefer to sell themselves on fear and disaster. Even in our conversations we tend to focus on what went wrong during the day and are less likely to name and celebrate the goodness we have received. We focus on fear and in so doing we depart from Don Bosco's positive approach and lose ourselves in a network of fear that he described as a repressive system. That repressive system, operating in our culture airbrushes kindness from life and leaves us all poorer as a result.

Yet psychology tells us that loving kindness activates the same parts of our brain that sex and chocolate stimulate! Not only that, kindness reduces the effects of ageing, depression and improves immune system strength.[1] So, whilst being kind to others has seriously positive effects on an individual, it can also create a stronger sense of belonging and of community. The second part will only be true if we learn to focus on the positive, the kindness and the understanding that we experience each day.

Which means that we need to notice that kindness has been shown. Remembering the experience and perhaps talking about it later avoids us airbrushing it from our own lives. That remembering of loving kindness brings it from below our personal radar and allows us to share it with family and community. In time we will learn to see loving kindness and share it more easily with others and perhaps resist the competitive fear that stalks many of our lives. Don Bosco created a space called the oratory which was safe from the competitiveness of the streets and businesses of a chaotic area of industrial Turin. Within the oratory he created a home, a playground, a school and a Church for young people. It was a school of kindness where the young people themselves received kindness and learnt to give it in equal measure.

Today that oratory atmosphere is needed more than ever. Every family, school and workplace can become a seedbed of loving kindness. This kindness is not for wimps—it takes courage to be kind because it makes you vulnerable. You may be laughed at or exploited or even attacked. Yet kindness challenges our individualised culture and can transform it from within. This is especially true for those who carry authority in the family, the school or the workplace. Terse, top-down instructions tend to create repression and resistance whereas kindness creates community. With community comes energy, self-sacrifice and healing. With repression, resistance and fragmentation are the long-term results.

Don Bosco's spirituality challenges every culture to build life around loving kindness. Partly that is because it works—it brings people to life. But more importantly Don Bosco realised from his early experience that in giving and receiving kindness he was in touch with the love that moves the world, a love which Christians call 'Father'. Don Bosco saw this Fatherly love everywhere and in the most ordinary acts of kindness, smiles and gestures of understanding.

---

1   M. Babula, *Motivation, Altruism, Personality and Social Psychology: The Coming Age of Altruism*, (London: Palgrave Macmillan, 2013).

Recognising that God was so close allowed Don Bosco to be cheerful and optimistic about even the most wayward young people.

10 Tips to Put Loving Kindness into Your Life

1. At the end of the day remember the good things that have happened.
2. Allow yourself to be cared for and praised by others and say thank you.
3. Notice how good and patient people are around you even if they sometimes aren't kind.
4. When people get into a moaning session distract the focus to make it more hopeful.
5. Tell people you appreciate them and praise them often.
6. Don't let your timetable become so rigid that you can't help out a friend.
7. Forgive other people for not being perfect and trust them with a fresh start.
8. Risk being kind to someone who seems a bit scary.
9. Pray for those who are having a hard time.
10. Be gentle and kind to yourself when things go wrong.

Don Bosco's Spirituality

Don Bosco wanted to provide four things for a healthy spiritual life:

> A Home.
> A Church.
> A Playground.
> A School.

Playground is the first and possibly the most important space, a place to relax. It is the place where you can be yourself, live in the present moment, develop relationships and be spontaneous. We all need that space in our lives because it is one of the places we meet the presence of God, in our play.

Home is a place where we belong, a place where we are accepted whatever has happened. It is a secure space, a warm and welcoming space. Everyone needs that through family or friendships for the whole of their lives. It is also the word that describes God: the place where we belong, our home.

Church is the community where people search for answers and meaning to the mystery of life. Each person has to have a place in their life where they can engage with life's meaning. They need a place to meet their God and find a deeper and longer perspective on their life through questioning and imagination.

School represents a regular space to reflect on the events of our lives and to learn from experience. It is a state of mind in which we can reflect on what we know and what we do not know. It can enlighten where we are going and discern the choices we have to make. It is a humble space where we recognise that we do not know everything.

RUAH

This is the Hebrew word for spirit and for breath. It spells out four key Salesian attitudes to relationships with others and with oneself. The four words are:

- Respect
- Understanding
- Affection
- Humour

Respect literally means "to look again". It is an invitation to look deeper, especially at people and see their dignity and their mystery as equal human beings. That means no exploitation, no sarcasm, no hurtful banter and no degrading of others or oneself because we are all children of a loving God.

Understanding is not just about knowledge but also about empathy: understanding experience from another person's viewpoint. Most people are hungry for understanding and, when it is provided, they flourish and learn to understand others. That is why guidance and friendship are essential for all people.

Affection is an expression of emotional engagement, showing kindness, sharing good news and expressing concern for others. Sometimes hurt makes us vulnerable to disappointment and it takes courage to be kind. All affection must be balanced within an atmosphere of freedom and responsibility. It requires self-discipline and maturity.

Humour is the safety valve for a healthy sense of self and relationships. For Don Bosco, being generally cheerful and optimistic was a sign of holiness. "We don't want any long-faced saints around here!" he would say to his community. Humour dissolves intensity and self-importance and brings perspective.

A Salesian Monthly Check-up

Once a month Don Bosco asked people to stop for a few hours and look back. It was a great therapeutic and spiritual experience for both individuals and groups. Here is a way of following that tradition:

- Fix part of a day near the end of a month when you have a few hours.
- Tidy up your personal possessions removing anything you no longer need and give it away.
- Return anything you have borrowed.
- Look at your diary over the last month and call to mind what has happened both good and bad.
- Talk to God about what has gone wrong and recognise your own fault.
- Resolve to apologise to anyone you have hurt and make a prayer of sorrow.
- Take the next opportunity to go to confession.
- Thank God for all the good that has been done and shared and resolve to thank those who have got you through the last month.
- Invite God to be with you in the month ahead remembering any challenges which lie ahead and asking for God's wisdom.
- Say an 'Our Father' and have a mini celebration!

This can be done as a solo exercise or as a family or as a group of friends sharing a house or a workplace. This kind of exercise done regularly begins to shape personal experience into a pilgrim journey that has both direction and meaning.

A Monthly Check-up List

Once a month find a few hours during the day and follow this simple pattern to tidy up your life. Slow down and review where you are with friends, family, life plans and God. Tick off the stages as you go. The timings are only a rough guide. Use some music you like to get you into the mood to tidy up and then to slow down and reflect. You could create a playlist for each stage.

Make sure you give your mind time to think back and let the significant memories emerge. Invite God to walk back with you through your month and discover together what really mattered.

Time	Task	✓
1st half hour	Tidy up your personal space—empty bins, identify/return things you have borrowed. Decide to pay back money you may owe.	
2nd half hour	Look at clothing and items you no longer need and bag them up to give away.	
3rd half hour	Look back thankfully over your diary, your messages and experiences. Ask God to bless those who have been good for you this month. Then think about mistakes, people you may have hurt and commit yourself to apologise to others and to your God.	
4th half hour	Reflect on the month ahead. How can you be different, grow in loving kindness and honesty? Make any changes in your timetable for the new month. Invite God to walk with you into the future.	
	Celebrate another month of your life! Invite a few friends to join you.	

Finally, celebrate the month and tell others what you are doing and some of the things you want to celebrate.

Balancing Your Life Like Don Bosco

Reflect monthly and quietly on these questions:

Have I found space to be silent and still?
When have I been moved by creation, kindness or
beauty? What moment has been sacred for me? What
sacred questions do I hold about my life now? When
have I felt touched or held by a presence larger than me?

Have I generally
kept cheerful?
How much time have
I spent on exercise,
hobbies, friends?

Church

What have I
discovered about my
world; myself; others?
Who has been my
best teacher?

When did I
really laugh or smile?
What am I looking
forward to?
What has kept me
optimistic about life?

Playground   **School**

Where did I get
stuck?
What do I still need
to learn?
For whom am I a
teacher or a guide?

Home

Where have I felt most relaxed, myself?
Who could I rely on? Who might have missed me?
Who have I missed? Where was my personal space?
With whom has there been intimacy—intellectually;
emotionally; physically?

Sharing Your Month with Friends and Partners

Can you share your deepest
desires and hopes?
Can you sense the deep goodness in your friendships?
Are there any 'holy memories' from your friendships?
In what ways are your friendships changing the world?

How honest are
we in expressing
personal needs?
How do we relax
best together?
What is the most
fun moment that we
have shared?
Has it been ok to
waste time together?

What have we learnt
about each other's
gifts?
Where have we
learnt about our
weaknesses?
In what ways
have we been
complementary?
What is the main
lesson our friendship
has taught us?

Church

Playground

School

Home

When was our best, relaxed shared moment?
When has understanding and trust been most visible
between us? Have we respected each other's personal
space? When has care been shown? When has care
been received gracefully?

Looking at Your Month of Experience through RUAH

Have you respected:
- The sacred mystery of your life and the lives of others?
- The limitations of people- including yourself?
- Creation, food, time, property and promises?
- The deeper wordless patterns moving in all relationships?

Have you lived cheerfully by:
- Maintaining a buoyant positive attitude to what life brings?
- Drawing on the deeper life-giving mystery of people?
- Staying with the flow and flexibility of life despite disappointment?
- Remembering the smallness of your life and laughing at yourself?

Have you lived with understanding by:
- Remembering that you are a learner, never closing your mind?
- Thinking through confused situations?
- Remembering your own joys and failures?
- Being steady and logical under pressure?

R
H U
A

Have you lived with heart by:
- Allowing emotion a place in experience?
- Engaging with others honestly and faithfully?
- Being open to receive and give affection?
- Showing gratitude and joy as much as sadness and disappointment?
- Expressing your anger in a healthy way?

Holiness

Holiness is too often seen as an escape from life and a narrow-minded way of seeing things. Nothing can be further from the truth. Holiness is all around us all the time. It is in the young person who cares for a struggling parent without complaint. It is in the footballer who will not give way to provocation and keeps calm. You will find it in the one who is always optimistic and cheerful even when times are hard. Holiness is doing the ordinary things extraordinarily well. Holiness is within reach of everyone. Pope Francis has written a whole letter about holiness, and he gives five signs of holiness. Pope Francis reminds us that these are not the last word on holiness, but they are outward signs that holiness is at work in peoples' lives. As you look at the list below let your mind go to the people in your own life. Who displays these gifts? How do they come out in their lives? Have you ever thought of them as holy? Would you consider thanking them for these holy gifts?

1. Perseverance, Patience, Gentleness.
2. Boldness and Passion.
3. Community minded living.
4. Constant prayer.
5. Joy and a sense of humour.[2]

"Do not be afraid of holiness. It will take away none of your energy, vitality, or joy."[3]

Salesians believe that everyone at any age and with any history can live a virtuous life. In other words, everyone can be a saint, including you. Each person's path to virtue or holiness will be unique because it will emerge from their life experience. Two clear experiences that signal the start of this journey are:

*   A sense of a presence within that reassures and accompanies all that is best in your life.

*   A driving force to do good for others wherever you might be.

Once you start to listen to these two aspects of your life you are already on the road to virtue and holiness. You begin an inner conversation between yourself

---

2   Pope Francis, *Gaudete et Exsultate (Rejoice and be Glad)*, March 19, 2018, Chapter 4. [*GE*].

3   *GE*, n. 32.

and the mystery that is God in your life. You sense that you are being drawn to act with compassion, to act for justice, to be optimistic about yourself and others and to be more cheerful, buoyant and resilient. You come alive!

Listening to that call to virtue moves you out of yourself to a more generous and reflective way of living. Your ego takes a step back to make way for self-sacrifice and kindness that opens up new depths to your relationships with people and with creation. You are on the way to being a saint! "We need a spirit of holiness capable of filling both our solitude and our service."[4]

Four Salesian Models of Virtue and Holiness

Below you will find four stories of young and virtuous lives arising from the Salesian network. Read the stories and reflect on the way your own story is unfolding. Look especially for the sense of a deep and compassionate presence within you and your desires to make a difference to the world around you. Notice how each of them reflected a unique mixture of the signs of holiness described by Pope Francis.

Michael Magone (community building and joy)

Mickey was a gang leader based at the railway station in Carmagnola, not far from Turin. He ran a number of money-raising scams around the travellers and was well liked by his gang members. He had no father, and a mother who had to work more than twelve hours a day. He went to school sometimes but was often noisy and disruptive.

He bumped into Don Bosco in 1858 at the station and Don Bosco recognised in his character a huge sense of fun alongside a really serious and thoughtful depth. Don Bosco asked him to see the local parish priest and get a reference. If he did that, his costs would be paid to attend Don Bosco's school in Turin.

When Mickey arrived in school, he was noisy, disruptive and slow to focus. Don Bosco had appointed a mentor for Mickey called Tom who soon realised that Mickey was haunted by his past actions. He persuaded Mickey to go to Don Bosco for confession and spiritual direction. Within a short time, all the roughness, anger and defensiveness fell away. Mickey became a hugely popular figure and was able to recognise his own selfishness and harshness.

---

4   GE, n. 31.

He had begun to develop his personal virtues. He became courageous, forgiving, generous and compassionate. Mickey died of tuberculosis at the age of fourteen. He died peacefully and even joyfully in the presence of Don Bosco and his friends.

Dominic Savio (joy and prayer)

Dominic was born in 1842. His dad was a blacksmith and his mother a seamstress. He was brought up to listen, to pray and to do his best in everything. Through family life and early schooling Dominic developed a strong sense of God's presence in every moment of his life. That awareness helped him to be optimistic and realistic about himself and he seemed to have a wisdom beyond his years.

Don Bosco heard about Dominic's goodness from a local parish priest and visited the family to see if he could support Dominic's desire to become a priest. Dominic exceeded Don Bosco's expectations in intelligence and spirituality, and he agreed to support his journey to priesthood. On arrival at Don Bosco's school, Dominic heard Don Bosco speak about everyone becoming a saint, that being a saint was easy and that happiness that comes from being a saint will last for eternity. From then on Dominic resolved to become a saint.

But he went about it the wrong way. He started spending long periods in solo prayer and even putting stones in his bed to make him suffer poor sleep. Don Bosco found out and told him that "here we make holiness consist in being cheerful". Don Bosco told him that it is as important to be in the playground as it is to be in church. He was balancing up Dominic's virtues and integrating them into a normal life. Dominic's sense of God's presence became so developed that he became aware of the needs of others without being told of them. On one occasion he informed Don Bosco that someone needed him because they were dying, and he gave Don Bosco the address. Dominic had never been to the house but was aware in some mysterious way. Dominic died before his sixteenth birthday already at a level of virtue that many adults would never achieve. He was made the saint of adolescents by the Church in 1954.

Laura Vicuña 1891–1904 (prayer and perseverance)

Laura was born in Chile and moved out with her family during a bloody revolution. Her father died of pneumonia soon afterwards. Laura, her mother Mercedes and her sister Julia became refugees and journeyed to Argentina.

There, Mercedes came under the control of an unscrupulous ranch owner who provided her with work and a home as well as education for her daughters on the understanding that she would share his bed. He turned out to be a sadistic bully sometimes branding women that he became tired of.

Laura and her sister were enrolled in a new Salesian school where they both grew in maturity and spiritual wisdom. But as she grew older Laura herself became the focus of the rancher's attentions. Unlike her mother, Laura resisted and took many horrendous beatings. The Salesian school supported both girls through this. Laura calmed her mind and heart through prayer and good advice at school and she prayed especially for her mother who lived hour by hour in fear of her life.

Laura made a promise in prayer that she would be willing to give up her own life to save the life of her mother and she mentioned this time and time again to Mercedes, her mother. Later Laura contracted tuberculosis and died on January 22, 1904. Mercedes eventually broke away from the abusive rancher and took her daughter to safety. The way that Laura managed such a troubled life and a painful death convinced many of her holiness. Her persistence, courage, cheerfulness and trust in God were never defeated. Here is one of her key thoughts: "You must know how to suffer and to forgive each other's failings, and love each other as good friends."[5]

Sean Devereux (joy, boldness and passion)

Sean was born in 1964 in England and attended Salesian College in Farnborough where he excelled in sports and entertainment as well as in academic study. Sean qualified as a teacher and went to work at Salesian School, Chertsey. He was happy to teach and enjoyed the role, especially the extracurricular activities put on by the school. However, inside him there was a deep and urgent pressure to use his skills and gifts for the neediest young people in the world.

---

5   *The Life Story of Blessed Laura Vicuña (Biography of Laura Vicuña).* Online: http://www.donboscowest.org/saints/lauravicuna [Accessed April 1, 2022]. Originally written in Italian by Sr Maria Domenica Grassiano, FMA under the title of *La mia vita per la mamma. Laura del Carmine Vicuña.* It was translated into English under the title of *For love of my mother. Laura Carmen Vicuña* by Sr Mary Doran, FMA. Cf., D. Madden, *A Greater Love: A Brief Account of the Life of Blessed Laura Vicuña,* (Bolton: Don Bosco Publications, 2020).

After a few years, Sean volunteered to go to Liberia in West Africa to work with the Salesian mission there. Liberia was in the middle of a long civil war, and it was a tense and dangerous place to be. Sean realised that the many street children had no opportunity to play safely and started putting on events that helped them to relax and form normal friendships. All sorts of concerts, competitions and sporting events were his strategy to break down the barriers of mistrust among young people.

Sean began to realise that many of the young people were being abducted as child soldiers and he put himself in harm's way many times by approaching rebel leaders to reclaim these young people from the drug filled violence that awaited them. He said: "While my heart beats, I have to do what I think I can do, to help those that are less fortunate."[6]

That became his mission statement for life. Later, because he refused to compromise with the rebel leaders in Liberia he was advised to leave. UNICEF invited Sean to help them with the feeding programme in a famine and war-torn Somalia. He became known for his fairness and kindness in the distribution of food. He would not give into the threats and pressure from local rebels. In the end he was shot from behind by one of the rebels in Kismayo. He died instantly. His work continues through his family charity, The Sean Devereux Children's fund.[7]

---

6   M. Delmer, SDB, *Sean Devereux: A life given for Africa*, (Bolton: Don Bosco Publications, 2004), 62. Cf., S. Seddon (ed.) *Sean Devereux: The Beat Goes On*, (Bolton: Don BoscoPublications,2017).
7   https://www.seandevereux.org.uk/

SECTION II

Your Own Life

Your Life: Just 700,000 Hours

The figure of just over 700,000 is not the salary you deserve. It is the average number of hours of life people will have before they die, assuming no accidents or serious illness intervenes. It's not that long, it's totally mysterious and as an adult of 20+ years a quarter of that life has already gone. It's never too late to take more control of your life and make sure you are looking after yourself physically, psychologically, socially and spiritually.

This section guides you through some major spiritual life themes and draws on the wisdom of the Catholic tradition and upon the insights of positive psychology.

Who Are You?

The Catholic Church believes that you are unique, precious, and personally connected to the eternal mystery of life. When you are amazed at beauty, when you fall in love or when you are full of gratitude for life, our Church believes that you have been touched by the mystery that many people call God. In fact, Catholics believe that you are directly and personally related to that mystery. You share a family likeness with God simply because you are human. Perhaps that is why Jesus asked us to talk to that mystery as 'Our Father'. So, Catholics believe that you are a child of God, full of dignity and with an eternal dimension to your story that is unfolding every day.

At times, you may feel worthless, overlooked and a failure. You may sense a dark pessimism in your life that seems so real and almost overpowering. There is more about that later. For now, it is enough to say that within that darkness of soul our Church believes that you meet something deeper and stronger: a presence and an unconditional love that invites you to trust and believe in your own goodness. However you may feel from day to day, Catholics believe the promise of Jesus that he will be with each of us personally and always, until the end of time.

Who We Are as Human Beings

We are part of a species that has evolved over millions of years into a thinking and feeling network of people reflecting the mystery behind all creation. We have broken through to an awareness that shares the mind and the heart that built the whole of the universe. We are connected, spirally bound through our DNA, into the mystery of life. We are also interconnected with all other people: we breathe the same air, share similar feelings, struggle with the same problems and enjoy exploring our lives and relationships as well as the world in which we live.

This interconnectedness is a vital part of your humanity. We grow and develop together and flourish in teams and families rather than as isolated beings. These bonds between people also seem to have a sacred side to them; friendships, marriages, promises and responsibilities all express that sacredness. Being loyal to friends and saying "I love you" to someone are sacred aspects of our humanity as a species. Without that sacred dimension of life, we cannot build sustainable living communities or families. The Catholic Church says this clearly in its funeral service, "The ties of love that bind us together in life are not broken by death." So, your relationships touch eternity, and they will last for ever. Deep down we belong to one another. We have never, ever, been totally independent individuals.

Why Are We Here?

The Catholic Church believes that we are here as part of a new generation of people who are exploring the mystery of life and community as pilgrim people. We have inherited many traditions of thinking and relating to the mystery of life. We know that many of the major religions approach that mystery in slightly different ways, but they all have a rich experience to share with us. We are here to continue to experience life, to build loving kindness, to explore life's meaning and to celebrate human dignity.

In doing those things we touch our deepest spiritual levels as individuals and communities. We get to know the mystery at work below the surface of life a little more. We start to develop a conscious relationship with a mysterious presence that is too big for our thinking minds. Our job is to listen to that presence and be guided by it in building a more just, more compassionate and more human society. We do that by trusting what is best within us and choosing hope, faith and love as virtues that connect us to the heart of creation. Catholics believe that they are not here to help themselves at the expense of others but to lay down our lives in the service of others. Catholics believe that in Jesus we can see a guide and an example of how to live as human beings and so the story of Jesus in the Gospels becomes a way of living and a pathway to meaning in life and to an encounter with the living God. Salesians are committed to helping young adults start that lifelong journey with their friends into the mystery of their being.

Being a Young Adult

As you enter active adult life, you bring with you a special responsibility to question what you see, especially if it seems to harm the dignity of human life. At this stage of your life, you need to test yourself to see how your strengths and ideas stand up alongside other peoples' ideas and strengths. You need to find where you belong. So, friendships, sport, travel, adventure, campaigns, and social groups will be your sacred ground for finding yourself and also making a difference to the world.

To that task you will bring some precious gifts to our world: your creativity, your energy, your skills, and your ideals. As a young adult you have not had to compromise, in the same way as older adults may have done, with ideals that are important. You will have the energy to be very focused on specific issues that may change your world. In changing your world, even in small ways, you also learn who you are and begin to get a clearer idea of who you are called to be and what you will need to do with your life. You will find your vocation calling you from that deep presence within you that Catholics call the Spirit. Be ready to stay in touch with that presence and allow it to guide you, through experience, towards a relationship that will give meaning to all your life.

Being Good News

You do not need to be more than a few years old before you recognise that all people are a mixture of good and not so good. People say things and do things that harm themselves and others. We develop destructive habits, and we sometimes teach them to others. As a young adult Catholic however, you are called to be good news for others. That means recognising that people carry many different types of damage that separate them from the deeper presence that gives meaning to life. But, while being realistic about people's weakness, Catholics are also permanently optimistic about their goodness too.

The Gospel challenges you to see and encourage goodness wherever you find it and to celebrate life's goodness whenever you can. The Gospel tells us that the best way to beat your enemies is to turn them into friends. It tells us that the way to encourage goodness is to praise it in others and overlook small faults as thoughtlessness. In being good news for others one of your greatest gifts is simply loving kindness. Sometimes the hard-heartedness in people is like a block of ice which is there to kill the pain of past hurts. That coldness allows people to be cruel to others without feeling any regret. Loving kindness helps to melt that ice and allows people to feel human again, admit their hurt and be healed, in part, by your compassion. Gratitude, praise, and encouragement can be used to awaken optimism and hope in all your relationships.

Being Yourself

We are all unique because of our genes and because of our history. We have gifts that come from both our parents, and we will carry some of their weaknesses as well. Part of our work as young adults is to recognise those gifts and weaknesses as we explore life. We have also had experience that has shaped our lives. We will be passionate about some things because of our experiences. For example, the experience of parents separating may make us passionate about family life. The experience of a musical family may have awoken a gift for music. We are an adaptable species and all of us have more potential gifts than can ever be developed. Life experience will have triggered some of those gifts early in your life but there will be more as you grow further into adulthood. So, listen for your gifts and recognise the gifts of those around you.

The Catholic Church believes that the mystery of God is at work in the stories that people are living each day and in all of history. Those stories and events become an opportunity to get to know that inner mysterious presence better. So, thinking through what happens to you can reveal two things: firstly, how close that mystery called God might be in your life and secondly, it can reveal more clearly who you are becoming. At a deep spiritual level, that mysterious God tells you who you are and calls you by your own name. When you touch that experience of being recognised by God's mystery your sense of dignity grows and so does a deep desire to be fully alive in that spirit. Your story then changes from being a series of random events into a journey deep into the mystery of life that Jesus spoke of as "Father."

Looking After Your Body

Catholics believe that God became one of us in the life of Jesus. He took on our flesh and knows what it is to be human, to be tired, to enjoy exercise, to run, to eat and to rest. Your body is described by Catholics as a "temple of the spirit"[1], a place where, in some way, the mystery of God's presence can be found. So as a young adult Catholic look after your body, not simply to attract others or to build your confidence but also to get to know that presence of Jesus that inspires your flesh and blood. Exercise and care for your body, give it rest, keep it clean and dressed with dignity because it is the place where you encounter the mystery of life.

Using alcohol and drugs in ways that dull your conscious mind can damage both your body and your soul. Anything that leaves you out of control can also lead to behaviour that is destructive and less than human. Yet, you are always responsible for your actions even when you are out of control. Conscious loving kindness for yourself and others is the pathway to wisdom and wellbeing. Try not to let alcohol and drugs rob you of that blessing. You need to give your body rest as well as activity. Sleep is essential to the spirit. Make room for play, it was Don Bosco's preferred pathway into the presence of God. Over-tiredness can lead to anger or depression and result in damage to your key relationships. Listening to your body is essential in keeping healthy, do not ignore the ache of tiredness or the need for exercise. Listen to those needs as a sacred message from an inner wisdom that cares for you. Love yourself and your body as an expression of your story and your personality. Try not to be drawn into the superficial comparisons of beauty that can destroy your self-esteem. We are told that only one person in three million has perfect physical features. Your beauty is not about shape or skin tone but about the spirit and the integrity that you carry, the spirit that shines through many different shapes and sizes and gives them soul.

Looking After Your Mind

Your mind is a treasury of unique memories that have shaped your soul. The millions of connections in your brain have been laid down year by year into patterns that make you different from everyone else. No one has quite the same view on life as you have. Your conscious mind is part of the mystery of

---

1 *Catechism of the Catholic Church*, (Vatican City: LEV, 1993), [*CCC*], n. 364.

life that science is still exploring. That science tells us that our minds change throughout our lives and are developing particularly rapidly until our mid-twenties. One of the last parts of our brain to develop is the pre-frontal region which damps down impulsive actions. That means that young adults are likely to make mistakes, misread situations and act inappropriately at times. Few mistakes are fatal, and they are the main way that we learn in life. You will develop a more balanced mind if you can stand back from these mistakes and reflect on what happened afterwards, when you are calm. That kind of thinking helps your mind to make better connections and to learn from the experience, making you a wiser and more contemplative person.

In the same way, when things go well, stop and think how your actions and intuitions led to good results. Allow those intuitive connections in your mind to get stronger. After each positive experience store a memory away of what has gone well. That will help you to counteract the pessimistic and disaster modes of thinking that can take over our minds and paralyse our lives. Those positive memories can also help to dampen down the anger and self-pity that can sweep through our minds and leave us with dark moods and even self-hatred. Above all, keep thinking and keep reading. Learn new things that stretch your mind whether that is a new language, a hobby or a sport, anything that keeps you alive and flexible in your thinking. Have experiences, as many as you like, but keep reflecting on them as well. Use techniques such as meditation, journaling, and mindfulness to calm your mind and notice how negative thinking patterns may be harming you. Learn to breathe slowly through anxiety and anger so that it does not overcome you. The sense of anger, misery, peace or happiness you feel often begins with a thought. So, look after your thinking. Have a look at the gratitude exercises later in this book and practise living positively each day.

Looking After Your Soul

We have been brought up in a world where nothing is real unless it is tested, unless there is evidence and proof. That is helpful for planning projects and measuring things but unhelpful in looking at people. Who can measure love for example? How can you prove someone is in pain or hurt? How do you analyse the depth of a friendship? You know you are friends with another person but all that might be seen on the surface is a smile or a pattern of meeting. Only those in that friendship have the evidence that proves it to be real. That is the kind of knowing which opens the mystery in people and reveals their soul. The soul is the place where a person is connected uniquely to the mystery of life that many people call God. It is a sacred space that makes us who we are and calls us home to ourselves.

Looking after your soul involves a sensitivity to the way in which we are moved by life's events. Catholics talk of listening for "that still small voice"[2] which whispers through our busyness. That inner voice can often awaken in us a deeper awareness which allows us to look beneath the surface of life and see the personal significance of events. Our culture is powerful in telling us how to think and how to fit in: you must be a financial success, you must be out on a Friday night, you must look fashionable and so on. Your soul on the other hand is asking you to choose how you want to live. It is asking what you want to build your life upon and how you want to make an impact on the world. Memory, imagination, silent meditation, and deep conversations all help to unmask the destructive pressures of drifting with the crowd and fitting in. Soulful reflection opens up the opportunity to choose life at the deepest level. Only your soul can guarantee your integrity and peace of mind and it is never too late to listen.

Relationships: being a friend

One of the most precious gifts we share as human beings is friendship. These privileged relationships, based on freedom, are vital parts of growing into fullness of life. Some of us need many friends and others are content with one or two friends. Friendship needs will vary according to your personality. For many, family relationships blossom into deep life-long friendships. There is no doubt that human beings flourish in a network of friendships and struggle when that network breaks down. Catholics believe that these friendships can be a mirror of God's love living in people. When we know that we can call a friend at any hour and they will make time, when we are understood and believed, when we are forgiven, we touch a deeper and sacred dimension to friendship. Then we see the face of God revealed in our own friends.

---

2   Read the story of Elijah and the cave from the Jewish Testament in 1 Kings 19:11–13.

The spiritual depth of love

The Catholic Church has always had a clear view that friendships and intimacy reflect the love of God living in people. "Love one another as I have loved you," said Jesus.[3] So, our love and friendship can be an intimate and spiritual experience of God as love. Jesus' words encourage us to treasure the gifts of touch and friendship as a way to experience God's presence. St Aelred of Rievaulx said "whoever abides in friendship abides in God and God abides in them."[4] Saint Aelred wanted people to find an abiding love, one that lasts through time and through tensions and creates a unity and a community where people can thrive.

We instinctively recognise the goodness of these abiding friendships and a long-term intimacy in life. Within the safety of such relationships, we can heal life's hurts, build confidence and embrace the fullness of life as we embrace love and friendship. But there is always risk and sacrifice in relationships: we have to learn to put the other person first and hope that they will do the same for us. This tug of love, giving and receiving, brings joys and challenges and it makes us human because we are never fully ourselves unless we are also interdependent. Scripture, in the book of Genesis, reminds us that it is not good to be alone (Gen 2:18). All our learning to live together is a preparation for learning to live with God in an eternal relationship. So, it's important to put friendships and intimacy high on the list of your priorities. This applies to everyone, to single people, to separated people, to priests and religious people.

Intimacy

Intimacy in western society is a word that has been hi-jacked to mean mainly physical intimacy, having sex, or making love. That is a part of intimacy but there is more to intimacy than just touch. Three aspects of relationship come together to give a unique shape to each person's experience of intimacy:

1. Physical—touching
2. Emotional—sharing feelings
3. Thinking—sharing thoughts and ideas

---

3 Read the Gospel of John 13:34.

4 Aelred of Rievaulx (1110– 1167), *On Spiritual friendship: The Classic Text with a Spiritual Commentary by Dennis Billy, C.Ss.R.* (Notre Dame, Indiana: Ave Maria Press, Inc, 2008), 41.

The Catholic Church has always wanted physical intimacy to be surrounded and supported by a "communion of life and love" where emotional intimacy allows a psychological nakedness to build a deep bond between people. The other element of intimacy, sharing of thoughts and ideas, provides the place where commitment can be made that is independent of touch or feelings but based on a clear and permanent choice to share life with another person.

One of the reasons why the Catholic Church wants these three elements in a healthy intimate relationship is because of the level of vulnerability and openness of the couple. When we put ourselves into the hands of another person, we need to be a partner and not an object. If we are touched in intimacy by another person as if we are an object, we are damaged spiritually. We need the security of compassionate mutual feelings and a mature long-term decisive choice to create that safe intimate space where no harm can be done. Intimacy is the space where the human person can be explored, healed, and celebrated.

The Catholic Church believes that God became one of us in Jesus. God has become intimate with human beings. We say: "The Word (Jesus) became flesh" (Jn1:14). So, as we touch the flesh of others we also connect with the mystery of God in the other. It is important to enjoy this gift and allow the ecstasy and the deeper emotion of faithful love making to become a sign of God's love living in people. When a couple are that closely committed then they become a kind of sacrament, an outward sign of God's faithful love for others.

A healthy friendship checklist

Friends are important to our flourishing as human beings. Sometimes we can be so desperate for friendship that we lose all perspective on our own needs. Friendships that began so positively can subtly move into an unhealthy pattern. Without realising, we may have handed over control of our life to another person, their opinions, needs and preferences can dominate our lives. In some senses we can lose our own soul in the process.

We can also adopt a domineering role in a friendship that can turn our friendships into a form of low-level bullying. In a prayerful way, reflect on your own friendships in the presence of God and use the checklist overleaf to review how you or they may be a source of health or harm. Be prepared to change and to talk honestly to your friends about what emerges from your reflection.

Healthy Friendship Checklist		
Healthy	**Where is this friendship moving?**	**Unhealthy**
Are balanced: both people give and receive from each other.		Are one-sided, draining energy from the other.
Are respectful of personal boundaries.		Are marked by pressure, sarcasm and criticism.
Encourage people to change and develop.		Struggle when one person changes their mind or feelings.
Do not cling but leave people free.		Become jealous or angry about wider friendships.
Build a person up, energising and enriching life.		Often create doubts and tiredness.
Meet you as you are without pressure.		Want you to change or fit in with their thoughts and plans.
Leave room for your own feelings.		Want to control or judge your feelings.
Are safe and honest places to be oneself.		Break confidences and undermine trust.

Your vocation: finding your direction

The average young adult will probably experience at least nine changes of role in their life journey, as well as some periods of unemployment. The range of choices faced by this generation are greater than they have ever been:

- Where do I live?
- What kind of long-term relationships do I want?
- Will I stay close to home or move away?
- What kind of job do I want to do?
- What do I do when people I relied on move out of my life?
- What is of ultimate importance to me?
- Should I travel and risk losing friends?
- When do I commit myself long term to another person?

All these questions hide deeper questions: What kind of person am I? Who do I want to become? What am I afraid of? What do I do with my deepest desires? To whom do I belong?

In all these questions the Catholic Church offers you not a series of answers but a person, Jesus, to accompany you from within on the path of your life. That pathway is not pre-determined. It is being made every day in the choices that you make. The South Americans have a saying: "a path is made by walking."[5]

It is in the action of moving forward that your unique path is made. On that path the Church offers you a friend and guide in Jesus and a Gospel so that you can make sense of what is happening and develop an inner conversation with the deep wisdom that the Gospel reveals. Your pathway will emerge at the place where your deepest desire overlaps with your world's deepest needs. A sense of vocation develops as your awareness develops. That awareness includes your memories, your relationships and above all an awareness of your own deep spirit, your soul. When these are given space in your mind and heart, are reflected on in the light of the Gospel and the needs of your world, then everything is changed, and the person of Jesus is revealed as your companion on the road.

---

5   A. Machado, 'Proverbs and Songs', in ID., *Border of a Dream: Selected Poems of Antonio Machado*, translated by W. Barnstone, (Washington, USA: Copper Canyon Press, 2004), n. XXIX.

So, your vocation puts you into the footsteps of Jesus as he brought his own deep desires in touch with the needs of ordinary people. He wanted them to have life and have it to the full (cf. Jn 10:10). That was his vocation and ours will echo that same desire in a different time and in your own unique story. "Only a life lived for others is a worthwhile life."[6]

Testing your Vocational Dream	
Is your dream easy to achieve?	If your dream is too easy, it will not stretch you or focus your energy. It must be a challenging dream.
If this dream did become reality what would change?	A dream has got to have an impact on the world and support the common good. It should not just go on in one's head or be self-centred.
Is this a family / friend's dream and not really yours?	Many people lose a sense of their own inner spirit and end up following the agenda of other people. This often looks like going along with the crowd or parental wishes.
Have you done anything about this dream so far?	Most dreams are already simmering beneath the surface and will have triggered some experience. If there is no experience a person might be fooling themselves.
Is it a dream that resonates with your life?	A good dream arouses passion and even anger in a person because of experiences they have had. If there is no energy like this the dream isn't mature.
With whom can you share this dream?	Dreams that stay in the head don't get the air they need to develop. In the end all good dreams are relational dreams.
Is this dream rooted in Gospel values?	Does your vocational dream reflect the Gospel of self-sacrificing love and the sacredness of life?

---

6   'Einstein Is Terse in Rule for Success', in *New York Times*, June 20, 1932, online: https://www.nytimes.com/1932/06/20/archives/einstein-is-terse-in-rule-for-success-only-life-lived-for-others-is.html [Accessed 29 September 2023].

Vocation: Discerning Your Gifts

A plumber carries a tool kit which supports their work of fixing pipes and keeping water flowing safely. Looking at a person's tool kit can tell you a lot about their work. In the same way, looking at personal gifts can help to clarify what a person is called to do with their lives. But the way you see your gifts can be distorted by pressures in life: you may be told that you are good for nothing by some people and others may give you unrealistic flattering feedback that sets you up to fail. That is why good faithful and honest friends are important. Listen to your spiritual companions for their caring honest opinions. Listen to your heart too. It is the place where the still small voice of the Spirit speaks. Notice how your energy grows and your focus sharpens as you think about different ways of using your gifts. Listening to this inner Spirit takes you into a mystical journey that connects your gifts and the world around you. So, your true gifts are found by reflecting on experience, honest friendships and listening to the Spirit as a kind of inner satnav.

It might help to look at some online surveys of giftedness to make sure that you have a wide grasp of your own giftedness. One of the best is the VIA Strengths Test based on a positive psychology model.[7] VIA stands for Values In Action and helps you to identify your best self and also your signature strengths. Try it along with a few friends and share your results.

---

7   https://www.viacharacter.org/ [Accessed 2 October 2023].

SECTION III

The Catholic Religion

Religion

Religion and personal spirituality sometimes seem quite different. In fact, they both need each other in order to be effective. Prayer, meditation, celebration and virtuous living are the places where spirituality and religion come together. This section explores how you might use religion and spirituality to strengthen your inner life. In this section you can learn to meditate and pray in traditional ways and also through more personal experiences. It introduces you to the mystery of sacraments, the daily prayer pattern and the tradition of building the common good in the world around you. Research over many years has shown that personal prayer and belonging to a religious community have a strong beneficial effect on meaning, purpose, happiness and health.[1] So, let's start by reflecting on the positive aspects of a healthy religion for your journey through life.

Healthy Religion

We live in an age of radical re-thinking about religion. Some see religion as a superstitious relic of older cultures. Others see it as part of a deeper search for meaning. Most religions began as radical movements trying to make sense of life in a new way. Religions are constantly developing and at times their thinking can become over-elaborate to the point where rules begin to smother the spirit of those religious traditions. Healthy religions develop their thinking as change happens. Unhealthy religions freeze their thinking and refuse to adapt and can become museums rather than a living and truth-seeking tradition. Here are ten tests you can use to identify a healthy religion.

Qualities of a healthy religion

- Begins with life and leads back towards fullness of life and is not always other-worldly.
- Increases awareness of your personal gifts as well as your frailty and compassion.
- Creates a sense of living in a flow of a presence at the heart of all life.

---

1   G. Rees, L, Francis, M. Robbins, *Spiritual Health and the well-being of urban young people.* The Commission for Urban Life and Faith, The University of Wales, Bangor and The Children's Society, 2006.

- Is motivated by faithfulness to an inner integrity rather than an unthinking acceptance of external rules.

- Increases moral strength to serve those in most need.

- Leads to an ongoing transformation often expressed as a personal journey shared in a community experience.

- Establishes a balance between inner reflection and engagement in life.

- Builds up a basic optimism about life and people, which leads to greater hospitality.

- Increases a capacity for love and self-sacrifice for others.

- Builds interdependence with people of all races and creeds.

If you find that your experience of religion is not too healthy you are in good company. Jesus often expressed frustration with some aspects of formal religion. He challenged religious leaders, yet he never abandoned his own religious practice as a Jew. In a similar way, most Catholics regard the Church as a mother. They are well aware that 'Mother Church' is not perfect, but it is still their mother, the place where they learned about life and its meaning. So, Catholics recognise in the Church a wisdom tradition that is slowly adapting to their needs whilst staying faithful to the Gospel of Jesus on which it began.

For that reason, a faithful Catholic is not one that blindly accepts all that the priest says but one who is also prepared to develop their conscience and to search for ways to be faithful to the Gospel today. It is only through the tension between tradition and change that the growing pains of a new Church can lead to new life. As a young Catholic, your task is to challenge the Church, love the tradition and stay within it rather than drift off into a shapeless spirituality. A privatised spirituality will not support your life journey or bring you into a deeper relationship with the Jesus of the Gospels. The Church needs you to rub the salt of young adult idealism into the compromises of a wounded adult Church.

Statues and Saints

The Catholic Church has had its own celebrity culture for many centuries. It offers real people as models of the way to live a good and holy life. You will see these in the form of statues and images around many churches. Each one has a story to tell, qualities to emphasise and truths to inspire our lives today.

They led heroic lives and yet they were not perfect, and Catholics do not worship such people but only God.

Signposts

The saints are signposts to living the Gospel faithfully and different saints seem to attract different people. Saints also come and go: when their story happens in a culture that seems strange to us, the power of their witness somehow diminishes, and they do not engage as much with Catholics today. Some saints seem to endure through thousands of years: St Francis of Assisi, St Benedict, St Teresa and St Patrick. They all seem to speak to our present age. Other saints have been removed from the Church calendar altogether, such as St Christopher.

Mary, Mother of God

The Mother of Jesus has always had a strong presence in the Gospel story, often in the background but consistently present at key stages in the life of Jesus. She represents a feminine thread in the tapestry of the Gospel. Pull that thread and you discover that she was part of a wider group of women without whom Jesus could not have done his work in Palestine. It is a pity that the culture of the time did not give more attention to this group of women who would have engaged in discussion and understood Jesus at least as well as his disciples. They were also the first witnesses to the resurrection of Jesus and the first to proclaim it to the world.

If you look at St Luke's Gospel and at St John's Gospel, you will see that Mary played a crucial role in the growth of Jesus as a young person and also in holding the disciples together after the death of Jesus. She is therefore called "The Mother of the Church." She was held in such regard in the early Church that it is believed that she went directly to join her son, Jesus, when she died. The Church believes that Mary still continues that role as Mother of the Church today. For that reason, you will often hear Catholics pray the Hail Mary when they begin meetings or have to make big decisions. Mary is a model of the way we can carry Jesus into all the situations that we meet. Don Bosco saw her as a helper in the spiritual journey to God especially for young people.

Catholics Making a Difference

People seem to be most alive and more themselves when they have discovered a sense of meaning in life and a purpose for living. Without these, a human being is likely to slip into despair or selfishness. Most people want to feel they have made an impact on life through work, relationships or creativity. Older people, looking back on their lives seem to be especially proud of what they have helped to create, not just physically with their hands, but also through relationships expressed in friendship and family.

Yours is a generation that is more aware than any other before it of the inter-dependence of people and the shortness of our natural resources. The world you can help to build will need to be more interconnected, caring, generous and consistent. Yours will be a generation that lets go of an unhealthy individualism and helps to build a new awareness of a world community. At the level of relationships, it will be a time when the sacredness of family relationships is nurtured and preserved. It will be a time of more cultural mixing and a deeper awareness of the human spirit. It will also continue be a zone of conflict, a battle for the soul of each person by the media, by the world of work, by consumerism, and by politics. Your generation are called upon to guard the dignity and worth of each individual and to save their souls.

The Church has always tried to go out and live the values of the Gospel to help to build a better world. In recent years that has been expressed practically in Catholic social teaching and the ideal of the common good. Many of these guidelines have been picked up by politicians to frame policies for a more just and compassionate society. They are not well publicised, and some people have described them as the Church's biggest secret.

Catholic Social Teaching

Being a practising Catholic is sometimes seen as going to Mass on Sunday. That is a travesty of the truth, there is much more to it than that. As Catholics, the Church asks us to pray every day and especially in the morning and the evening. It expects us to act morally and to love God and our neighbour in the practical business of getting on with life. One of the best ways to spell out what that means to be a practising Catholic is through Catholic social teaching. This approach encourages us to live out six themes in all our work and relationships as a way to build a better world. Some Catholics who attend Mass regularly on

Sundays can sadly ignore these six themes and only appear to be practising Catholics. The themes of Catholic social teaching follow.

Human dignity

If we want to build a better world, we must recognise we are all brothers and sisters. That spiritual connection requires us to respect, value and uphold a common dignity for ourselves and each other. As human beings Catholics believe that we are created in the image and likeness of God so therefore we have an inherent worth and dignity as individuals and as communities.

Community and participation

As humans we were not created to live alone, community is clearly linked into the history of our species. One way for Catholics to practise solidarity is to participate in pursuing the common good for a community. Every member of society has a duty to develop this common good and every member has a right to enjoy the benefits brought about by it. This means having an approach to life that is more "us" than "me." Jesus modelled that solidarity in His acceptance of all, rich, poor, women, men, children, local people and foreigners.

Care for creation

Respect for human life means respecting all of God's creation. We must re-engage with our environment and take responsibility for it; live sustainably, live so that there are enough resources for everyone. Our environment influences almost all our lives, and Catholic social teaching recognises that undervaluing our world makes us all poorer economically, socially, and spiritually. Pope Francis wrote a long letter to the world, *Laudato Si'*. He said, "We have forgotten that we ourselves are dust of the earth our very bodies are made up of her elements, we breathe her air, and we receive life and refreshment from her waters."[2]

Dignity in work

This theme looks at the importance of work, the dignity of work and the value of balance in our home and working lives. Catholic social teaching holds that work is not to be drudgery, but creative, positive and an intrinsic good. It is not however, a way to accumulate power and influence, but it is rather to play our part in being co-creators in God's loving act of creation.

---

2   Pope Francis, *Laudato Si'*, (May 24, 2015), n. 2.

Peace and reconciliation

The Church teaches us that peace is central to the Gospel and represents a challenge to many contemporary attitudes and assumptions. Pope Benedict XVI challenged Christians to be true peacemakers bringing forgiveness and non-violent solutions to situations of hurt and violence. Much of the tension that leads to division and violence comes from the inequalities between groups that build up a deep sense of injustice. Peace makers need to work both at the level of individual divisions and at the level of systems which have become self-centred and unjust.

Solidarity

Solidarity is an important concept for Catholics and is one of the most mystical and deeply human founding concepts of the social teaching of the Church. It is based on the belief that together we can make a difference and together we are much stronger. When we value fellow human beings, we respect each other as unique individuals and we can stand up for what is right for one another. Solidarity reveals a deeper bond in people that goes beyond race, gender, culture and religion. We are related to every other person and share a common responsibility. Or as the Bible reminds us, we are our brother's keeper (Gen 4:8–10).

The Common Good

The common good is a core idea coming from Pope John XXIII in 1961. It is the sum total of all the social conditions which help people to grow into fullness of life. It is not the greatest good for the greatest number because that might leave some deprived or rejected groups who do not share that fullness of life. Instead, the common good excludes no one and as long as one person is deprived, the common good cannot be achieved. The common good is based on a deep respect for human dignity and the sacredness of each life. Yet the common good also reminds us of our interdependence and of the demands of the Gospel that inspire us to work for the good of all. Even our property, our goods, need to be put at the service of the common good. It is immoral for Catholics to have a huge excess of goods when other human beings are in desperate need of them. Catholics are called to live simply.

Social Action

There is no authentic Christian who does not reach out in compassion to those in need or reach out in justice to those who are oppressed. Christianity is a flow of God's life and love to others and if it becomes self-centred, it dies. That outreach can be achieved through vigorous social action or by the faithful self-sacrifice for those in one's own family and neighbourhood. Jesus reminds us through many parables that our neighbour is everyone we meet and that we must love our neighbour as we love ourselves.

When you have spare time from your immediate duties it is good to look at the needs around you. Notice the ones that rouse your compassion or anger most strongly and reflect on why they seem more important to you. It could be that they remind you of your own story or they could be calling out gifts that you have kept quiet about. These movements of your heart are the beginning of a call, a vocation, to act in harmony with the Gospel and to build a better world where God's goodness flourishes in every person. Christians call that better world the 'Kingdom of God'.

Being a member of a Church opens up many ongoing projects that you may be drawn towards: Saint Vincent de Paul groups serving the isolated and lonely in your area, CAFOD groups campaigning for justice world-wide, Mary's Meals responding to hunger, homeless projects, refugee projects and so on. Many of these projects work quietly and locally and may not have a high profile. You may need to seek them out and engage with them. If you feel at home with the people you meet, and with their aims, you may also have found companions on your pilgrim journey through life.

Sacraments: Not Magic, But a Deeper Reality

Sacraments are most simply described as an outward sign of inner grace. There is an outward sign, such as the bread at Mass, that becomes an interior grace, a free gift of God's own presence. The outward sign of every sacrament is a way of focusing our awareness so that a deeper reality of God's abiding presence is revealed. The Church, over its thousands of years of experience, has identified seven sacraments that can authentically uncover the reality of God's presence:

1. Baptism
2. Confirmation
3. Reconciliation
4. Communion—Eucharist
5. Marriage

6. Ordination

7. The Sacrament of the Sick

Each sacrament is an invitation into a process that moves us from death to life. Even the sacraments which are received only once (Baptism, Confirmation, Marriage and Ordination) are the start of a process in living a life of loving kindness and self-sacrifice in the footsteps of Jesus. From the first splash of water in Baptism to the final touch of oil at the anointing before death, the sacraments connect us to the mystery that lies at the heart of the universe and to the life of Jesus. These outward signs of an inner relationship open up meaning and direction for every human life.

There is more: each sacrament opens an Easter pathway through life experience into the presence of God. Each stage of life and each event involves a letting go and a receiving of something. Each event contains a dying and a rising, a cross and an Easter. Receiving the sacraments puts us back in touch with this deep mystical pattern and presence in our lives. It reminds us of Jesus' words "I am with you always, until the end of time" (Matt 28:20).

Sacramental Imagination

Catholics have always had a strong feeling for visualising the mystery of God. You can see that expressed in the church services that use candles, colourful vestments, stained glass and incense. The visual helps us to connect to the mystery of God that always goes beyond words. At a personal level, each Catholic is challenged to look at their world through the eyes of Jesus. That means seeing what is happening through the Gospel. When you see one person helping another you are actually seeing the Gospel in action once again: the parable of the good Samaritan is being repeated (Lk 10:25–37). When you see a person pushed aside and ignored you are seeing the lepers whom Jesus saw and embraced. (Matt 8:1–4) The Gospel and sacramental imagination work together to transform your view of life. In that personal view you may feel that you too are called to be a good Samaritan, to reach out to the stranger and follow your own unique path to fullness of life. A Catholic who knows how to use sacramental imagination is able to recognise the deeper realities of life in everyday events.

The Eucharist—Mass

The Eucharist is a remembering and a celebration of the life, death and resurrection of Jesus. It focuses on the way that God is present in our lives:

- In the people as we gather.
- In the scriptures as we listen together.
- In our shared remembering of the sacrifice of Jesus on the cross that led to resurrection.
- In receiving the bread of Jesus' real and risen presence.

That living, dying, and rising happened thousands of years ago but Jesus is present at every Mass now in his people, in his Word and in the bread and wine offered again on the altar.

The experience of Jesus following his Father's Will and refusing to deny that relationship led him to death and through death, to a risen life. That story moving through life to death and to resurrection will unfold on your own life journey as well. The pattern of growth and decline will be part of your lived experience. Catholics call it 'The Easter mystery'. For that reason, the Church does not teach that Jesus has risen, the Church teaches that Jesus is risen. The pattern of his life, his desire to do good, his trust in his Father was stronger than death and Jesus is now present in all time and for all people. Sharing the Eucharist is a meeting with the risen Jesus. It is a chance to recognise his presence in our own life patterns of growing, living, struggling, and dying that we all face every day in many ways. Those experiences put us alongside Jesus and become our unique path of the cross and resurrection.

Therefore, the Eucharist can take every experience you have and fill it with hope and meaning. Every Mass is celebrated in time and out of time and Jesus is really present to everyone, speaks to everyone and gives himself to everyone as food for their journey. Even if the singing is terrible, the homily boring and the church cold the Mass still achieves its purpose through your participation. It is you who bring your life, share with other people and reflect on what your life is about. The priest is there to make the Mass a valid celebration, but the Mass belongs to the whole congregation—it is the work of the people.

So, look deeper into the Mass, remember that this is what people have done for thousands of years: when children are baptised, when weddings take place, when people die, before battles, on anniversaries and before executions. The Mass marks the milestones of our lives with meaning but also with an eternal presence of Jesus as a companion on the journey. Look around the church, at the congregation, and contemplate where they might be touching cross and resurrection. Notice their faith, their perseverance and the network of relationships that surround you. Notice what words of scripture stick in your mind and receive them as a message or a question from God to you personally. And, when the priest raises the bread and wine, remember that it is also your life he is offering to God so that God's plans and presence can deepen in your life. When you go to receive communion, put out your hands and receive the consecrated bread as Jesus, made small and vulnerable for you to touch. Do not be afraid to touch Jesus, he is your most intimate companion, and he holds you in his own hands in just the same way. And when you eat that bread notice that there is now no distance between you and your God. You are in communion with God.

Reconciliation—Confession

The Catholic Church has used confession in at least two ways throughout its history. It was used as a way to bring back into the early Church those who had betrayed their baptismal promises when others had stayed faithful and died for their beliefs. Becoming a penitent, confessing your sins and taking on life-changing penances was the cost of returning to the Church community, many of whom had lost family and friends who had stayed true until death to their Christian beliefs. In that setting the priest operated as a judge, listening to the circumstances and then assigning penances. In the early Church those penances were severe such as living as a beggar, selling all one's property, becoming a hermit and so on. Later in Church history people began to go to confession not just because of major faults but because they wanted to live more perfectly as followers of the Gospel. In that situation the priest would listen, give advice and help them with their prayer life and resolutions. The priest became more of a spiritual advisor and the penance he offered became more like a doctor's prescription, to re-balance and strengthen the moral and spiritual life of the penitent.

Both aspects of reconciliation are still present in the experience of confession today. The priest is there to remind us of the forgiveness of Jesus, the damage we may have done that needs repair and to guide us forward in our spiritual life. The process of talking, sharing prayer and compassionate listening and absolution are the outward signs of the inward grace: the presence of Jesus. When the priest extends his hand to offer forgiveness, it is done in the sure and certain hope that God is more compassionate and more understanding than we are. Yet God is also persistent in inviting us to deeper awareness of his self-sacrificing love and to the fullness of life.

Do not be too worried about approaching a priest for confession. It is always a privileged part of their role and a conversation that it is totally confidential without any exceptions. Priests have died rather than reveal what they have heard in confession. It is one of the safest places in the world to speak about your darker experiences and thoughts and to have another person hear, understand and assure you of God's forgiveness.

Going to Confession

You will find that many churches offer confession on Saturday evening, often before the evening Mass. In other churches, you will see them advertised as 'by appointment'. That means that you may have to approach the priest and request confession. Normally the priest will agree to hear your confession immediately if that is possible. The other common setting for confession is during reconciliation services which usually take place in Advent as a preparation for Christmas or in Lent as a preparation for Easter. In this case a number of priests are available and are spread around the church in quiet spaces. Many people find this setting easier but there is often a lack of time to have an extended sharing.

When you begin your confession all you need to say is: "Bless me Father, for I have sinned". The priest will then ask you what is troubling you and try to understand the challenges you face. He will then remind you of the presence of God and share some of the wisdom of the Church and of scripture about your way forward. You will then be asked to make a prayer of sorrow for any hurt that you have caused or suffered and for any breakdown in your relationship with God. You will find an act of sorrow in the confessional area and in the appendix of this book.

The priest will then give you a penance, a practical action that will put you back on the right path. Sometimes this action will be aimed at restoring what your actions have broken: returning something taken, asking forgiveness of someone you have hurt. Other penances are aimed at building good habits such as daily prayer or abstaining from something harmful.

Confession is an experience of the forgiveness and loving kindness of God who understands our weakness but yearns for us to embrace the fullness of life and to help others to do the same. You enter confession aware of your imperfections and you leave reassured of your goodness and ready to grow into the image of a loving God.

Reading the Gospels

The Gospels are the core of Christian scripture and tell the story of Jesus' work. Christians see these Gospels as inspired and a way of meeting Jesus. When we read a letter from a friend, there is a sense in which they are present to us, and we are present to them. When we read the Gospel, we meet Jesus and Jesus meets us where we are on our own journey. So, reading the Gospel is a sacred meeting, a relationship, with the mystery of God. When you engage in a relationship you find yourself stirred by reactions to the other person, there is a feeling response. When you listen to another person you learn, you understand and begin to see things through their eyes. Reading the Gospels is the same, you react, you engage emotionally, and you learn to see the world with new eyes, the eyes of Jesus.

You will already know a lot of Gospel phrases- "going the extra mile", "lost sheep", "prodigal son" and "pearls before swine". All these are found in the Gospels. As human beings we are wired to receive wisdom through stories and much of our media is focussed around making and sharing stories. In the Gospel we have a collection of stories that carry the sacred wisdom of Jesus and through these stories you meet Jesus face to face. When you read a Gospel story therefore, you need to listen to your own response: how do I feel? With whom do I identify? What questions does this provoke in me? Using your imagination to enter the story and allowing it to happen around you can lead you to engage with Jesus and perhaps begin a conversation with him. That sacred conversation can link the Gospel story to your own life experience and to the presence of the risen Jesus. There is something quite intimate and revealing about reflecting on Gospel stories, they become a mirror for your own soul. The scripture reveals Jesus to you, but it also reveals you to yourself!

When you sit and read a Gospel story, do this:
- Find a quiet space and some time to stop.
- Invite Jesus to be with you through what you read and your reactions to it.
- Read a short section of the Gospel slowly.
- Stop and notice your first reactions and questions, sit with them for a while.
- Read it again slowly.
- Invite Jesus to show you what it might mean for you.
- Notice if you feel the need to change something about your life.
- Thank Jesus for his presence in the Gospel and in your life.
- Get on with your life more aware of the presence of Jesus.

You can search for Gospel stories on a web search using titles like:
- The lost sheep—being confused and dependent.
- Prodigal Son—coming to your senses after isolation and failure.
- Good Samaritan—taking risks for others.
- Parable of weeds and wheat—being gentle with imperfections.
- Parable of the talents—trusting one's own gifts.
- Cure of a leper—reaching out to those on the edge.
- Feeding of five thousand—sharing leads to miracles.

The Beatitudes: A Guide for Life

In the Gospel of Matthew (chapter five) you can read the eight Beatitudes. The word 'beatitude' means both blessing and happiness, and Jesus attaches deep blessings and happiness to eight key approaches to life. Some people see this as an action plan for Christians and others also see it as a kind of self-portrait of Jesus himself. In these eight statements, Christians believe that we find a way to become more like Jesus and to uncover God's presence in other people. This Gospel chapter is also the core of Catholic social teaching, a way of living and acting that respects the deep dignity of every human being.

Study these eight statements in the beatitudes octagon below, apply them to your life situation and you will find you are living the Gospel in practical action.

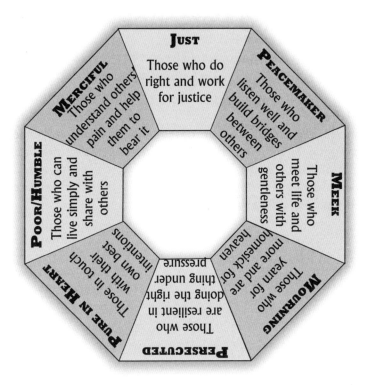

When you look at these eight statements, you will find that you are already living some of them instinctively. Others you will find harder to embrace. The good thing is that there are some aspects of your humanity in which you are already like Jesus. Even better, there are some areas where you need to struggle to be truly human. That pathway, from your strong points into your weaknesses is a journey of faith and so the beatitudes can become a map of your personal development as a daughter or son of God. This kind of reflection should lead you outwards from your strengths, to follow your vocation and make a difference to your world. It will also lead you inwards to recognise your need for others through the weaknesses you will always have in life. You will find a Salesian version of these Beatitudes at the front of this book.

Prayer and Personal Reflection

Prayers

Saying prayers is an important part of the Catholic tradition. Spoken prayer stands alongside the more individual meditational forms of prayer as equally important. Speaking prayers aloud or in your own mind brings a clear focus to prayer. Because they are known by others, these prayers can be shared as part of a community experience in church or in the home.

The prayers that follow are many and varied. Some are traditional, and others use a more familiar language. Some will suit you and others might irritate you. Try to find the prayers that work for you: ones that bring you closer to God and those you are praying alongside. You are free to write your own prayers too, especially when you are raising a family.

Praying Continually

St Paul reminds us that we should pray "continually" (1 Thess 5:17), which means that he must have a very earthy idea of being aware of the Spirit of God in all that we are doing. He was recommending a kind of awareness that parents have for their children, or two lovers maintain for each other even at great distances. The Catholic definition of prayer is really simple; prayer is raising the mind and the heart to God. It can happen in ecstasy or pain in routines or in new experiences, in the bath or in the bar. It is how we focus our mind and our heart so that we can share our lives with God who promised to be with us all the time (Matt 28:20). So here are some times you might be able to raise your mind and heart to God:

- Waiting for a bus
- Sitting in a traffic jam
- Waiting for water to boil
- During a sleepless night

- Walking to work
- Doing exercise
- Cooking a meal
- Cleaning
- Gardening
- Writing Christmas cards
- Watching people prayerfully

In each situation slow down your breathing, focus on what you are doing but also be aware that you are not alone. Use your imagination to visualise a deeper presence, an awareness within you. Raise your mind and heart to that mystery that many of us call God.

General Guidelines for Prayer in Life's Gaps

These are the natural spaces for prayer for a Catholic. But what do I do in these spaces when I want to make them prayerful? Here are some more detailed guidelines to help you get started.

1.   **Be in the present moment**—keep bringing your mind back to where you are and what is happening in front of you. Your mind might drift back to memories or ahead to what is happening but gently bring your thoughts back to the place you are in and appreciate it.

2.   **Use some imagination**—try to see things as if for the first time, the food you are cooking, the bus you are sitting on and notice things. Use your imagination, if you are worried about someone imagine that you are walking with them: what would you say, what would they say? On a bus imagine you are sitting next to God in silence and perhaps talk a bit.

3.   **Persevere with inviting God**—be present in your routines each day so that your mind is enlightened and your heart raised. By doing so, your world will open up with new depths and a deeper awareness of an abiding presence at the heart of life.

Techniques to Help Prayer

Arrow prayer / mantras

These can help some people to build up a deeper awareness of God by repeating a simple phrase. Catholics have used a variety of these prayers over the years:

- Jesus, Mary and Joseph, I give you my heart and my soul.
- Lord, have mercy on me.

I would encourage you to find your own mantra for the journey, something that seems to resonate with your experience and is rooted in the Gospels. For many years, when I was going through a lot of difficulties my mantra was "Lord, I trust you". For many months, it was the only way I could pray. Find your mantra either from the list of scriptural phrases on pages 82–83, or adapt one to your unique setting. Mantras tend to become part of you and can change over time. Many people discover a "signature Gospel phrase" that seems to catch where they are in life and that becomes their mantra.

Beads

Many religions have used beads to help people to pray. The earliest use of prayer beads can be traced to Hinduism, around eight centuries BCE. This practice was adopted by Buddhists and Muslims, and in the thirteenth century, Catholics began to use prayer beads as the 'Rosary' to remember the significant events of Jesus' life that are called 'the mysteries of the rosary'.

Any practice that has endured for nearly 4,000 years has to have some innate wisdom within it and prayer with beads has a lot to offer:
- It is simple
- It involves moving the beads which gives a visible and a physical focus
- It has a rhythm that focuses the mind
- It has a start and finish
- It can be done anywhere

The traditional Catholic rosary consists of one *Our Father*, ten *Hail Marys* and a *Glory Be* to the Father. This decade of ten Hail Marys is one of five in the prayer, so Catholic rosaries have sixty beads attached to a crucifix. Each decade has a Gospel focus such as the resurrection or the birth of Jesus. In this way the rosary becomes a journey through the life of Jesus and a way to deepen a relationship with God. You will find more detail on page 73.

Creating your own rosary

The beads can also be used in more personal ways: taking a decade to pray for each member of one's family, using it to count mantras, taking a decade to pray for each continent, using the beads to count one's blessings. All of these can help to integrate life and deepen our awareness of God in the ordinary moments of our day. Holding beads for some people is very reassuring and a liberating routine from the worries of daily living. I know some people who have made a rosary out of ten beads that they can wear as a bracelet. That means that they always have their prayer beads with them and can use them anywhere by just running the beads through their fingers.

Personal litanies

Litanies are listings of prayers or statements addressed to God to which there is a simple repeated response. A litany produces a rhythm of praying through repetition. Often only one word or phrase sticks in the mind from many phrases. That word or phrase is one that may resonate with your life and when it does you can stop the litany and reflect on why that word catches your attention. For Catholics, that word sticking in your mind is a nudge from the Spirit saying, "let's talk." Examples of contemporary litanies can be found later in this section.

Contemplation—A Cloud of Unknowing

Prayer is always a mystery because it involves our relationship with the mystery of all of life. In the fourteenth century, an English mystic, whose name we do not know, described prayer as entering a "cloud of unknowing". He said that it was the way we meet God, not by knowing but by allowing ourselves to be known. Just allowing God to look at us. There are many links between his work and the wisdom of the Eastern meditation traditions. He lived in the East Midlands of England and only seventeen copies of his book were made, and yet his inspiration bridges the years and holds the key to personal reflection for us all.

This kind of prayer is called contemplative prayer and it involves emptying the mind completely and simply being in the present moment. The prayer involves letting go of all distractions and gently putting aside the stream of random thoughts that occupy our minds. This is a tough but rewarding prayer. It needs practice and many of the techniques of Sufi and Buddhist meditation reflect the same wisdom and discipline. It takes time to build the strength to do this type of prayer well and perseverance is needed. Here is what the author of 'The Cloud of Unknowing' says about it:

In the beginning, it is usual to feel nothing but a kind of darkness about your mind like a cloud of unknowing. You seem to know and feel nothing except for a loving intent toward God springing from the depths of your being. This dark cloud will remain between you and God. You will feel frustrated, and your mind will be unable to grasp anything. Learn to be with the mystery of God within this darkness. Return to it as often as you can. To see and feel God in this life must always be done from within this dark cloud during prayer. However, if you strive to fix your love on Him and forget everything else, I am confident that God will bring you to a deep experience of Himself.[3]

Such prayer brings together two lovers, God and your own soul. Therefore, go after experience as well as knowledge of God. Being clever and full of knowledge about spiritual things can inflate your pride and separate you from God. Instead, accept that you do not know and allow the gentle loving affection of God to touch your soul. That love will bring you to rest and to a knowing that goes deeper than words. You will also be walking in the footsteps of great mystics like St Francis, St Teresa, Meister Eckhart and many other Catholic saints.

Breathing as a Prayer

Breathing has been described as the doorstep of deep prayer. The Hebrew word for God is said to be unpronounceable and can only be breathed. The breath is important in meditation and prayer because it can help to calm the constant flow of ideas and help you to enter into the present moment. That is the place where you will meet the mystery of God. There are many ways to use breathing to slow down and there are some examples in the prayers section later in this book.

For now, why not try this simple approach based on the word spirit in both Hebrew (*Ruah*) and Arabic (*Ruh*). It is a word that sounds like breathing out (ru) and breathing in (ah). It is also the word for breath and for a breeze. The slow repetition of this phrase on the out breath and on the in-breath gives a focus to the mind and the body. As you slow your breath down it also helps to relax the whole body, increases the oxygen supply to the brain and allows you to escape the disappointment of the past and anxieties about the future. At the

---

3   Anon, *The Cloud of Unknowing,* translated by William Johnstone, (New York: Doubleday Image Books, 2005), 72.

physical level this breathing activates the parasympathetic nervous system, the body's natural antidote to stress hormones that can overwhelm our minds and bodies in everyday life.

After a few minutes of breathing like this you will become distracted. Don't get frustrated. Just gently put the distraction aside and return your mind to breathing out slowly (Ru) and breathing in slowly (ah). Say the two parts of the word in your mind as you breathe. Close your eyes or focus on a candle and let God look at you and be with you. That's it! At the end, thank God quietly for the gift of the time and invite God to stay with you when you have no time to pray or think.

Retreats

The Catholic Church inherited, through its Jewish roots, the importance of a day of rest each week. It was meant to be a quiet day, to stop all work and be a little more reflective. That need is still there in a heightened way in our fast-paced culture. The Church has chosen Sunday for this day of rest because it is the day of the week when Jesus rose from the dead. So, Catholics are expected to have a 'mini retreat' each Sunday which would include Mass and a time together with family. It is a day when families can find space for reflecting together on the week past and the week to come and for parents to bless their children as they grow.

From time to time, Catholics also take days or even longer periods for retreat. This practice breaks the normal routine completely and allows extended time to slow down and to contemplate what God might be saying through life experience and the scripture. In a retreat centre there is usually someone to guide you through the experience. But a retreat is first of all an intention to make space and slow down to re-connect with God. You can decide to take a long walk, visit a country park and talk to God as you walk. Parishes sometimes run retreat days in local religious communities especially in Lent and in Advent. They provide talks, opportunity for confession and a more intimate experience of Mass in a smaller setting. There are also opportunities for longer silent retreats in religious houses. In the UK and Ireland, you can google the retreat association to find where and when you can make a retreat.

SECTION IV

Prayers

Common Catholic Prayers

The Our Father is the prayer Jesus taught to his disciples and so it holds a special place in all Christian prayer. It reminds us that we are brothers and sisters, that God is holy, and we are dependent upon each other for food and forgiveness.

> *Our Father, who art in Heaven,*
> *hallowed be Thy name;*
> *Thy Kingdom come,*
> *Thy will be done*
> *on earth as it is in Heaven.*
> *Give us this day our daily bread;*
> *and forgive us our trespasses*
> *as we forgive those who trespass against us;*
> *and lead us not into temptation,*
> *but deliver us from evil. Amen*

The Hail Mary is a prayer that was addressed by the Angel Gabriel to Mary. It reminds Catholics of the way that Jesus became one of us, through Mary as his mother. The second part is a request to Mary to help us as we try to make Jesus present in our lives and our world.

> *Hail Mary, full of grace. The Lord is with thee.*
> *Blessed art thou amongst women,*
> *and blessed is the fruit of thy womb, Jesus.*
> *Holy Mary, Mother of God,*
> *pray for us sinners,*
> *now and at the hour of our death. Amen.*

The Glory Be is a short prayer of thanksgiving that reminds us that we are in the flow of life that we call the Trinity that will sustain us all forever.

> *Glory be to the Father,*
> *and to the Son,*
> *and to the Holy Spirit,*
> *as it was in the beginning,*
> *is now, and ever shall be,*
> *world without end. Amen.*

The Angelus is an old Catholic prayer that is traditionally said at 6am, midday and 6pm in the evening. It is designed to mirror the longer prayers of monasteries at these times. It was often timed to be said as the monastery bell rang for these prayers. The prayer reminds Catholics that Jesus became flesh and blood like us to be close to all people. It is usually said by a leader, and all respond with the part marked as R.

> *V- The Angel of the Lord declared unto Mary.*
> *R- And she conceived by the Holy Spirit. (Hail Mary....)*
> *V- Behold the handmaid of the Lord.*
> *R- Be it done unto me according to Thy Word. (Hail Mary....)*
> *V- And the Word was made Flesh.*
> *R- And dwelt among us. (Hail Mary....)*
> *V- Pray for us, O Holy Mother of God.*
> *R- That we may be made worthy of the promises of Christ.*
> *Let us pray. Pour forth, we beseech Thee, O Lord, Thy grace into our hearts; that we to whom the Incarnation of Christ Thy Son, was made known by the message of an angel, may by his passion and cross, be brought to the glory of his resurrection through the same Christ our Lord. Amen.*

Grace at meals is a tradition that has echoes in all major religions. It is a moment to stop and say thank you for the food we eat. It is a remembering that we are dependent upon the fruits of the earth for our lives and a recognition that they need to be shared with all people.

Grace before meals

> *Bless us, O Lord, and these Your gifts, which we are about to receive from Your goodness, through Christ our Lord. Amen.*

Grace after meals

> *We give You thanks almighty God for all Your blessings, who lives and reigns, world without end. Amen.*

An act of sorrow

When things go wrong, when harm has been done to others or oneself it is healthy to make an act of sorrow. All of us fall short of the high ideals of the Gospel and accepting responsibility for our failings is the way to be sure that we are not overwhelmed by them. An act of sorrow always focuses on the unconditional love of God for us, his people. That gives Catholics the confidence to admit their weakness. Use the one below or compose an act of sorrow in your own words.

> *God my Father, I am sorry for my sins with all my heart. In choosing to do wrong and failing to do good, I have failed in my friendship with You, whom I should love above all things. I firmly intend, with Your help, to repair the harm I have done, to choose a more loving path, and to avoid whatever leads me to sin.*
>
> *Our Saviour Jesus Christ suffered, died and rose again through trusting You; help me to do the same and walk more closely with Jesus on his Gospel path. Amen*

The Twenty Mysteries of The Rosary

The twenty mysteries of the rosary follow the events of the life of Jesus. For each mystery, one Our Father is said followed by ten Hail Marys ending with a Glory Be. The prayer is said rhythmically and in unison with others with a short pause after each mystery. It is usual to pray one group of five mysteries at one session. The prayer usually ends with one of each of the three prayers for the Popes intentions.

The Joyful Mysteries

1. **The Annunciation**: The Angel Gabriel announces that Mary is to become the mother of God's own Son, Jesus.

2. **The Visitation**: Mary visits her cousin Elizabeth, who is pregnant with John the Baptist. The two women recognise the Holy Spirit at work in their lives and their bodies.

3. **The Nativity**: Jesus is born as a person like us, closing the distance between God and human beings.

4. **The Presentation**: Mary and Joseph bring Jesus to the Temple where they meet Simeon who recognises Jesus as the one who will save us all from meaninglessness.

5. **The Finding in the Temple**: After losing Jesus in the temple crowds, Mary and Joseph find the young Jesus talking with authority to the temple leaders and they are disturbed by this strange behaviour.

The Luminous Mysteries

1. **The Baptism in the Jordan**: The voice of the Father is heard calling Jesus, "His beloved Son."

2. **The Wedding at Cana**: Jesus changes water into wine at a friend's wedding; this is seen as one of the signs that he was destined to change the whole of history.

3. **The Proclamation of the Kingdom**: Jesus calls all people to believe the Gospel and to change their lives and relationships.

4. **The Transfiguration**: The disciples have a spiritual experience, seeing Jesus overwhelmed in light and in the glory of God.

5. **The Institution of the Eucharist**: Jesus breaks bread at the Last Supper with his disciples, making a new commitment to people which would be stronger than death.

The Sorrowful Mysteries

1. **The Agony in the Garden**: Jesus endures extreme stress and fear as he faces arrest and promises to trust His Father in Heaven.

2. **The Scourging at the Pillar**: Jesus is scourged with whips to appease the religious leader of the time.

3. **The Crowning with Thorns**: Roman soldiers crown Jesus' head with thorns and make a mockery of him as 'King of the Jews'.

4. **The Carrying of the Cross**: Jesus meets his mother and falls three times on the way to the hill of Calvary.

5. **The Crucifixion**: Jesus is nailed to the cross, forgives his enemies and dies with his mother and the apostle John standing at the foot of his cross.

The Glorious Mysteries

1. **The Resurrection**: On the third day after his death, Jesus astonishingly rises from the dead.

2. **The Ascension**: Jesus gathers his disciples and ascends to heaven leaving them to continue his work.

3. **The Descent of the Holy Spirit**: The disciples, gathered in fear, receive the Spirit of energy and courage in the form of tongues of fire in an upper room with Mary the Mother of Jesus.

4. **The Assumption**: Mary is taken up into heaven by God at the end of her life.

5. **The Coronation**: Mary is crowned with a special honour because of her unique role in the life of Jesus.

Alternative Ways to Pray with Beads

Take a decade for each member of your family and think of them with gratitude and compassion.

Take a decade for each of the last few days. Let you mind run back through the day and ask to be shown what lessons and blessings each day brought to you.

Take your prayer around the world by praying for each of the five continents and their needs.

Look at different aspects of creation as a focus for a decade. Things like rivers, oceans, air, forests and cities.

Take a good friend and think about each of their good qualities as you pray each decade. You might choose their fun, compassion, integrity, gentleness, wisdom and so on and give thanks for all that they are to you.

When facing exams take your notes and place them in front of you. Place your hand on the notes and close your eyes and slow down your breathing. Using the beads repeat a phrase from the list below.

- I am with you always.
- Peace be with you.
- Do not be afraid.

Morning and Evening Prayers

Daily prayer is encouraged by The Catholic Church for all people. Prayers are especially important because they mark the start and end of the day and so connect the whole day with prayer. Morning prayers are usually short at the start of busy days. The evening prayers are longer and encourage a prayerful reflection on what has happened and where God may have been at work in your day. It is traditional to say a 'Hail Mary' or an 'Our Father' or a 'Glory Be' before or after the following offerings.

Short morning offerings

1. Father of creation, I offer you this new day of my life. Walk with me through all that will happen. Open my ears to hear your voice guiding my steps. May I walk in a gospel path and come home tonight with your will done, your kingdom built up and our friendship forever deepened. Amen.

2. Lord, I offer you this day with all the promise and uncertainty that it contains. I offer you all my fears and hopes for the day. Be the peace at the centre of my life today. Be the hope that survives each event. Be with me in all that happens. Amen.

3. Lord, I offer you this day as a holy space in which your heart and mine can share all that happens. I offer you all my hopes for this day and all the frailty that I bring to life. Speak to my heart in its strength and weakness and help me to build your kingdom of love and justice in the hours that lie ahead. Amen.

4. Lord, I offer you the journey I make today. May it be woven into your eternal plan of love for all creation. Let me walk alongside others with eyes wide open to the ways your love might link our journeys together. In affection and in argument help me to weave your life into all that happens between people today. Amen.

5. Lord, I offer you this day and all that it will bring. Anchor my day deeply in your presence. Steady my heart and mind when emotions within and challenges outside threaten my peace of mind. Take this day and let your will be done. Amen.

Evening prayer

In the evening Catholics are encouraged to make an examination of conscience; looking back at the day and seeing what lessons the day may have taught us. This is a peaceful process that may also lead to making an act of sorrow if we find we have done any harm. Here are twelve sample questions that might help with this first part of the prayer. Just one of them might lead you into reflecting on your day.

1. Have I found myself cutting corners and doing things too quickly?
2. Have I cut people off mid-sentence in the rush to move on?
3. Have I been hard on myself when things didn't work out?

4. Have I been hard on others when they have not performed to my standards?

5. Have I been gentle with creation, with work tools, with food and friends?

6. Have I been gentle with God's presence in me and others?

7. Where has love been offered today? Where has it been rejected?

8. Where has my own heart been moved with kindness and compassion?

9. Was I able to respond when my heart was moved in that way?

10. Have I allowed myself to receive kindness, affection, praise and belonging?

11. What can hold me back from receiving loving kindness from others?

12. How do I stand in relation to God's presence right now?

As these questions provoke your memory, invite Jesus to walk back with you through the day. Ask him to show you what the significant things were, the greatest blessings and the most important lessons. Allow yourself a good space for silence, then make a final offering prayer (choose one from below) before you sleep.

Evening offering prayers

1. Lord, I offer you this day. With all its routine and disappointment, it is the holy ground on which I walk with you, my God. Thank you for the shared journey of this day. Gather up what is of value and help me to let go of what is not worthy of me as a child of God. Amen.

2. Lord, you have walked with me today as a friend and guide. I offer you the successes and failures of this day and ask you to help me notice your guidance tomorrow. Show me how to follow the map of the Gospel and feel the tug of your Spirit drawing me in the right direction. Amen.

3. Lord, I offer you the best and the worst of this day. Take it and make it part of your cross and resurrection story and part of the Gospel pattern in my life. Help me to trust you tonight with the things that don't make sense and keep me patient with myself. Amen.

4. The day you gave is almost over, Lord, and I return it to you with gratitude for all you have achieved through my success and through my failure. Help me to see the promises of resurrection beneath the surface of even the most lifeless moments of the day. May I live by faith that your resurrection will eventually reach every corner of my life. Amen.

5. Lord, I offer you this day and the strands of your Spirit that have run through each moment. Thank you for your intimacy in my life and the daily

opportunity for partnership with you. Take the unfinished work of this day and use it all to build a better world. Amen.

Eucharistic Adoration

The Blessed Sacrament, the bread, which is consecrated at every Mass, is not all used at the Mass. Some is reserved because it may be needed to take to the sick at short notice by eucharistic ministers. It is kept safe in a locked tabernacle and usually there is red light lit to show that the sacrament is in the tabernacle.

Over the years many devout Catholics began praying in front of the tabernacle as a focus for the presence of Jesus in the sacrament and in their lives. When groups began to gather to do this, the sacrament was brought out of the tabernacle and placed in a stand called a monstrance so that people could contemplate, face to face, the mystery of Jesus' presence in their lives.

During adoration the main experience is one of silent prayer and people are encouraged to look at the monstrance and recall Jesus' request to remember him especially in the breaking of the eucharistic bread. During the adoration time someone will generally lead the group in short prayers, litanies, songs, chants and scriptural readings so that the silence is broken to allow some community prayer and praise. Many of the individual approaches to prayer mentioned in this book can be used in the silence of the adoration time.

The most solemn time of adoration in the Church year happens after Mass on Holy Thursday when the parishioners gather in silence until midnight.

The Practical Side of Going to Confession

This is a sacrament of healing and forgiveness usually called 'reconciliation'. That means being reconciled with your life in the presence of God and reconciled with others. Don't be afraid to approach a priest to ask for this experience. It is a sacrament that celebrates the fact that God's love, healing, and forgiveness is greater than any harm that has been done.

Here is the process:

- Make the sign of the cross with the priest.
- The priest may then say a prayer for you or share a short Gospel phrase.

- Then say: "Bless me Father, for I have sinned".

- Tell the priest if you have been to confession recently, or not for a long time. Don't worry if you can't remember the priest will not judge you. Knowing helps him to listen better.

- Then speak to the priest about:
  - ✓ Things that are weighing on your conscience where you may have hurt others by your words, by your actions or by negligence.
  - ✓ Talk to the priest about any damage you may have done to yourself by your lifestyle and choices that you may have made.
  - ✓ Talk about your experience of the presence of God as a friend. Do you feel God is close, or distant? Caring or demanding?

The priest may then ask you a few questions to check that he has understood clearly what you are saying. Then he will give you some simple guidance on how to work more closely with God in your life and ask if you are truly sorry for the things that have gone wrong, for the mistakes and hurt that you have done to yourself and others and to your relationship with God.

He will ask you then to make an act of sorrow for your sins. You can do that in your own words or use the one below.

> O my God, I thank you for loving me. I am sorry for
> all my sins, for not loving others and not loving you.
> Help me to live like Jesus and not sin again. Amen

The priest will then give you a penance. He will ask you to do something specific to begin a new pattern of life. It may be to say a Hail Mary, or a rosary. But he could also ask you to restore something you have damaged, apologise or return something you have taken. It is a small act to show that you really want to begin again, which the Church calls a firm purpose of amendment: a sign you really do want to change.

Finally, the priest extends his hand and says a formal prayer of forgiveness, often called absolution, on behalf of the whole Church asking that God forgive you and give you a fresh start.

Personal Litanies

Here are some samples of contemporary litanies which invite the person reciting them to count their blessings and to nurture a sense of gratitude for life. More traditional litanies are available on Catholic websites, and you are encouraged to create your own litanies of life to help you to pray more personally. Focusing on gratitude is also a fine way to combat the sadness that takes hold of us all from time to time.

Litany of gratitude for friendship:

	Response
	Thank you

For people who really listen:
For those who keep their word:
For those who keep confidences:
For friends who remain loyal:
For friends who tell me the truth:
For people whose shoulder I can cry on:
For those who never pressurise me:
For those who don't take over my life and freedom:
For the ones who always raise my spirits:
For the ones who make me think again:
For the ones with whom I am totally relaxed:

For those who invite and include me in their lives:
For those who endure my moods with patience:
For those who know my inside story:
For those who can forgive my thoughtlessness:
For those who trust me with their worries and hopes:
For those who help me to celebrate life:
For those who set me free to be myself:

All: Glory be to the Father, and to the Son, and to the Holy Spirit, as it was in the beginning, is now, and ever shall be, world without end. Amen.

Our Father, Hail Mary, Glory Be.

Litany of gratitude for family

For parents who have given me gifts and challenges:　　　　*Thank you*
For the home in which I grew up:
For learning through arguments:
For forgiveness shared:
For gifts exchanged:
For times of special togetherness:
For strong memories—good and bad:
For meals shared:
For illnesses and care shown:

For sadness shared:
For quiet spaces at home:
For wider family links:
For grandparents and their wisdom:
For self-sacrifice:
For jobs done and treats shared:
For gifts and surprises:
For being accepted by family members:
For the joy of coming home:

All: Glory be to the Father, and to the Son, and to the Holy Spirit,
as it was in the beginning, is now, and ever shall be, world without end.
Amen.

Our Father, Hail Mary, Glory Be.

Litany of the Holy Trinity

The Holy Trinity describes God as a community of life flowing between Father,
Son and Spirit. This litany is a prayer that I may be caught up into that flow of
life and energy every day.

God my Father,
God the Son, my brother,
God the Holy Spirit, my inspiration,
Holy Trinity, One God, have mercy on us.

Father from whom all things come,
Son through whom I am called to life,
Holy Spirit in whom I am being healed,
Holy and undivided Trinity, have mercy on us.

Father everlasting,
Only begotten Son of the Father,
Father, my Creator,
Son, my Redeemer,
Holy Spirit, my Comforter, have mercy on us.

Trinity that draws me into the flow of life,
Trinity that holds me in the mystery of love,
Trinity that teaches me self-sacrifice,
Trinity that moves within my being,
Trinity that moves the cosmos and creation, have mercy on us.

Trinity that draws me into joy,
Trinity that draws me into truth,
Trinity that helps me to receive,
Trinity that shows me how to give,
Trinity that leads me into mystery,
Trinity that teaches me to trust,
Trinity that helps me walk with Christ,
Trinity that helps me hear the Spirit,
O Blessed Trinity, have mercy on us.

All: Glory be to the Father, and to the Son, and to the Holy Spirit,
as it was in the beginning, is now, and ever shall be, world without end.
Amen.

Our Father, Hail Mary, Glory Be.

Closing prayer

Father, Son and Spirit. You called me into life to share your work of creation
and service of others. Help me, day by day, to grow into a family likeness with
you, to live in the flow of life and to walk with you each day on my journey of
life. Amen.

A Breathing Prayer

Breathe in with God's own breath of life,
Breathe out your worries and stress.
Breathe in God's love and acceptance of you today,
Breathe out your troubles and fears.
Breathe in the loving kindness of God,
Breathe out your fears and frustrations.

Pause

Sit quietly before the God who made our universe,
Breathing life into all creation.
Breathe in the presence of the one who knew you before you were born
And loves you to bits,
Be still before the mystery of your life and your God.

Pause

Breathe in with the breath of God,
Breathe out tightness and stubbornness.
Breathe in the gentleness of God,
Breathe out your pride and plans.
Breathe in the life of God,
Breathe out your loneliness and fears.

Now allow God to look at you.
When distractions come, gently push them aside,
Return to your breathing and become still.
Allow God to surround you,
And talk to you beyond words and hold you in mystery.

Daily Blessings

Blessing is an ancient form of prayer that calls for God's holiness and approval, friendship and support for a particular person, object or situation. Jewish and Islamic faith use the same word '*barakah*' for this type of prayer. Probably the oldest blessing in continual use for well over 3,000 years is found in the sixth chapter of the book of Numbers:

> May the Lord bless you and keep you;
> May the Lord make his face shine on you
> and be gracious to you;

> May the Lord turn his face towards you
> and give you peace (Num 6:24–26).

The tradition of blessing in recent years has been seen as something that is done by an ordained priest. It has not always been so. Isaac is described in the book of Genesis as blessing his son (Gen 27:27–29). Fathers are often asked to give their blessing to the marriage of their children.

The catechism of the Catholic Church says that: every baptised person is called to be a "blessing," and to bless[1] and especially where a person has a natural leadership of a group, occasional blessings would seem appropriate. Therefore parents, teachers, nurses, counsellors, doctors, married partners and so on should be encouraged to pray for God's blessing for those in their care. Parents especially are encouraged to give a blessing to their children together or individually before bed each night.

Sample Blessings

These sample blessings that can be adapted and used in various situations.

1. Lord, look with love upon _____. Fill them with the gifts of your Spirit, full of love, joy, peace, patience, kindness, goodness, faithfulness, gentleness and self-control. Keep them safe in your love now and always. Amen.

   Based on Galatians 5:22–23

2. Bless _____ with your presence Lord. May they do good, be rich in good works, be generous and ready to share, storing up treasure in heaven and doing good with their life. Amen.

   1 Timothy 6:18–19

3. _____, may the grace of the Lord Jesus Christ, and the love of God, and the friendship of the Holy Spirit be with you always. Amen.

   2 Corinthians 13:14

4. _____ , God loves you very much. He has lavished His love on you and has called you one of His own children. May

---

1   CCC, 1669.

you trust your God every day and be sure that you are loved now and always. Amen.

1 John 3:1

5. _____ , May God bless you with patience be quick to hear, slow to speak, and slow to anger. So that the peace of God may always find a home in your heart. Amen.

James 1:19

6. Lord God, you said that if we learn to trust in you, we would find perfect peace. Please bless _____ with enough trust in you to bring a deep peace despite all the troubles they face. Be with them in their challenges. Amen.

Isaiah 26:3

7. May God be with you all so that you may be kind to one another, tender-hearted, forgiving one another, as God in Christ forgave you. Amen.

Ephesians 4:32

Gratitude Prayer Exercises

When in desolation remember consolation was the advice given to Christians in the early Church. In other words, when your mood dips count your blessings! Move your focus to what is going well; as St Paul advised the people of Philippi, think about anything that is worthy of praise (Phil 4:8). Here are some exercises to help you to do that. Notice how you feel before and after having followed these exercises slowly and prayerfully.

Memory exercise

Go back to a moment in your life when you were most happy, most yourself, most alive. Remember where it was, when it was, what you were wearing, what the weather was like and so on. Remember who was there what you saw and how you felt. Stay with the feeling and thank God for that time. Ask God to show you what goodness came through that experience and allow that goodness to fill you up and strengthen your life for the future.

Looking in a focused way

Find something that is part of your life, that you take for granted and look at it in detail. Choose something that you normally take for granted. Notice the design, the colour, the wear and tear, the texture and overall shape. Thank God for this ordinary humble part of your life and ask God to give you a grateful heart for everything and everyone you will see today.

Looking at people

Notice someone in your life whom you know fairly well. Remember what they look like, how they sound and behave. Allow some of their qualities to surface in your mind. Remember them with loving kindness and list their gifts in your mind as you remember your experience of them. Resolve to give them some praise for their goodness as soon as you can.

Looking at yourself

Look back at your recent experience and remember conversations where people have said good things about you. Add those memories to the moments when you were caught up with something delightful, beautiful or pleasantly surprising. Keep the focus on everything about you that is good and wholesome and thank God for the way he has created you and called you into life.

Write a letter of gratitude

Make a time to sit and write a letter to someone to whom you are grateful. They could be family, friends, people in your past or even people who have died. Spend some time thinking about them and their kindness, inspiration, courage and so on. Write a note of thanks for all they have been for you. Read it through and thank God for this person's presence and action in your life. Then, you can choose to send it to them or just keep it as a reminder of the goodness of others.

APPENDIX

Don Bosco:
A Saint's Advice

Words of Wisdom from Don Bosco

Salesian spirituality invites us into a relationship with God's presence, especially as that presence is found in people. Don Bosco tried to raise awareness of God's love moving between people in order to create a healthy family spirit in schools, workplaces and the home. The best way to appreciate Don Bosco's spirituality of relationship is to read through some of his words about how people get along together. Behind all these quotes is Don Bosco's certainty that God, present in each person's heart, is the master educator.

- It is certainly easier to lose one's temper than to be patient, to threaten rather than reason with others. It often suits our lack of patience and our pride to hit back at those who resist us, rather than bear with them firmly and with kindness.

- Correction of friends should be done in private and in an atmosphere of care for the individual. Never start a personal confrontation in public except to prevent damage to others.

- I have rarely seen any advantage gained from lashing out at others without thinking first and before other means were tried.

- Let it be seen that no other rules are required than those that are absolutely reasonable and necessary.

- Even after the greatest of arguments with others, always leave open the possibility of forgiveness and a new beginning.

- To forget the unhappy days of a person's mistakes and to cause them to be forgotten by others, is the supreme art of a good teacher in the school of life.

- You can get further with a friendly look, with a word of encouragement that gives new heart and courage than with repeated blame which serves only to upset and diminish enthusiasm.

- I have often noted that people who demanded silence, impose high standards and exact prompt and blind obedience were invariably the ones who showed little respect for the useful advice given by wiser guides.

- People who never forgive others are often in the habit of forgiving themselves everything.

- Whenever there is a need to confront a person or an issue, great prudence is required. First of all, wait until you are in control of yourself; do not let it be understood that you are acting because of a bad mood, or in anger. In this event you demean yourself and the other person too.

- Everyone recognises that it is only reason that has the right to correct them. Therefore, make your demands upon others reasonable.

- Why do people want to replace loving kindness with cold rules?

- When people are thought of as superior to others, they are feared and little loved. And so, if you want to be of one heart and mind, for the love of God, you must break down this fatal barrier of mistrust and a replace it with a spirit of confidence. How do you break through this barrier? By a friendly and an informal approach with people, especially in shared free time. You cannot have loving kindness in your relationships without this familiarity, and where it is not evident there can be no confidence. If you want to be loved, you must make it clear that you love.

- The more you act from spite, the less you will be listened to.

- Let us rid ourselves of all anger when we must challenge others. No commotion of spirit, no scornful looks, no hurtful words on our lips. Instead, let us feel compassion for what is happening and offer hope for the future.

- One does not cultivate a plant by harsh violence and so one does not help people who struggle by burdening them with a yoke that is too heavy to bear.

- Someone who knows that they are loved will love in return, and one who loves can obtain anything.

- Confidence in relationships creates an electric current between people. Hearts are opened, needs and weaknesses made known. This confidence enables us to put up with the weariness, annoyance, the ingratitude, and the troubles which people sometimes cause. Jesus did not crush the bruised reed nor quench the wavering candle. He is your model.

- Remember that learning in life is largely a matter of the heart. God is the master educator, and we will be unable to achieve any lasting good unless wisdom teaches.

- The heart of every person is like a fortress which is always closed to rigour and harshness. Let us strive to make ourselves loved, to inculcate a sense of duty and a fear of doing harm. Then we will see the doors of many hearts open with great ease.